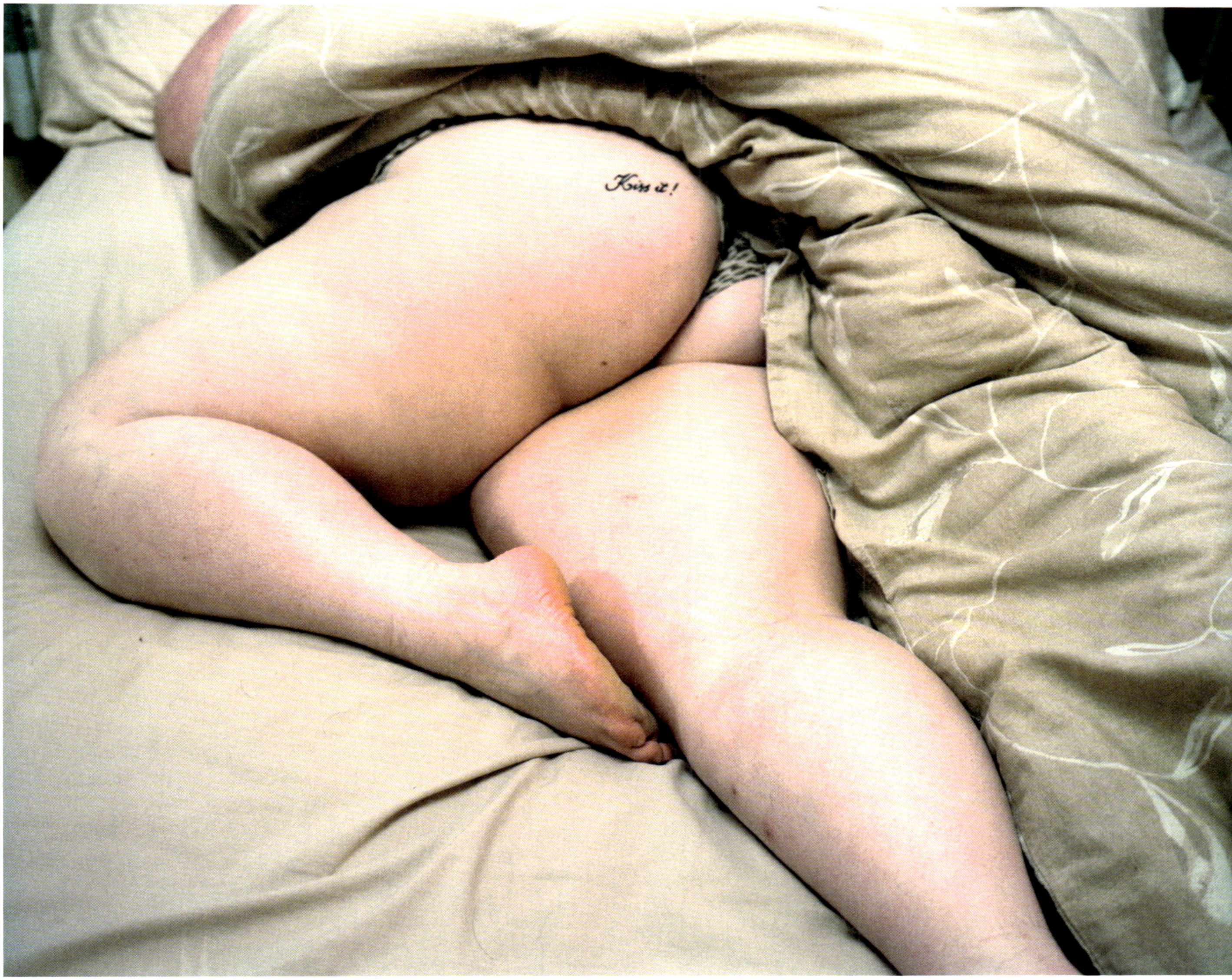
Kiss it!

2

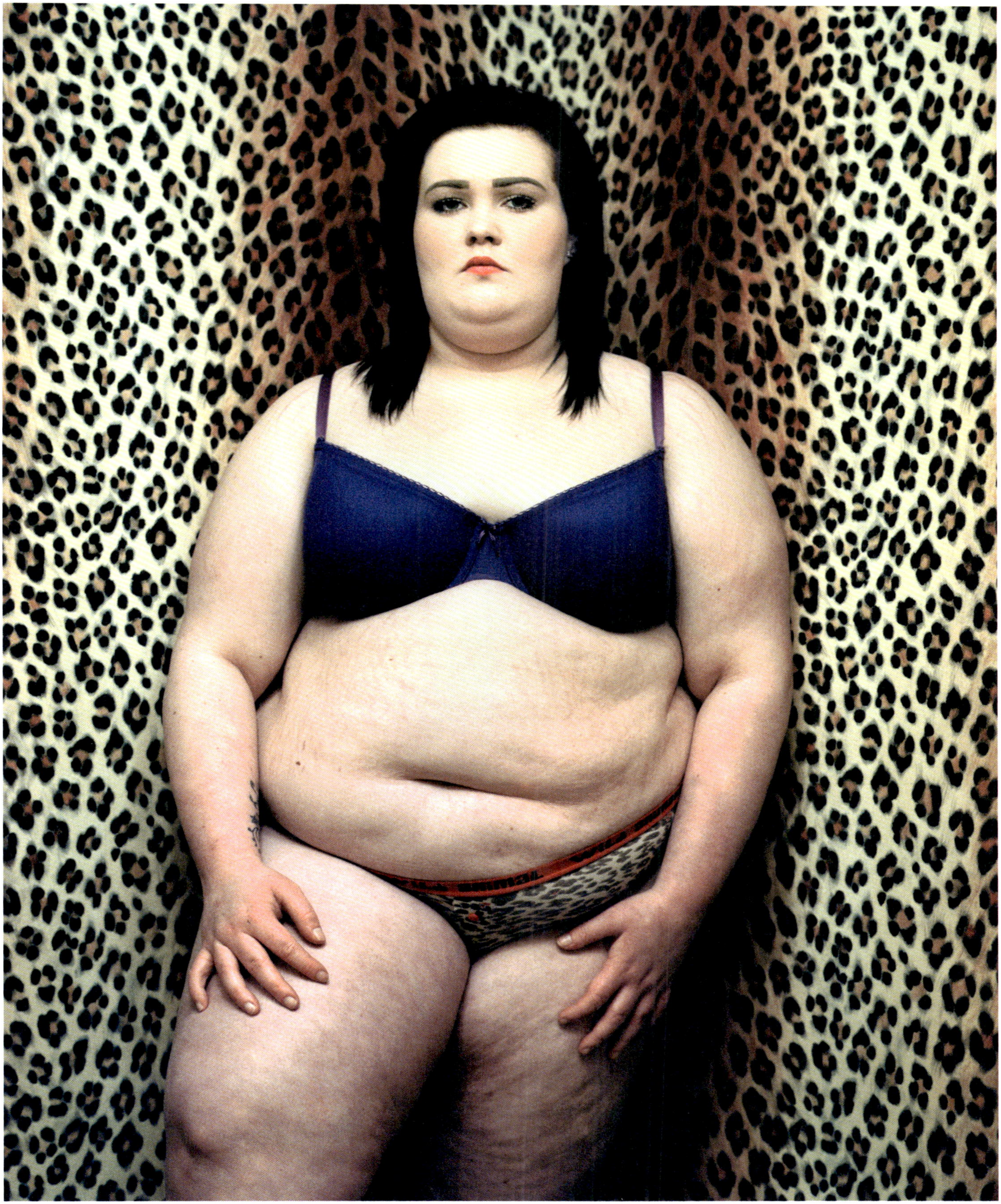

11. No more hassle from mum + dad, they would be proud of me instead of being ashamed.
From *Reasons to Lose Weight*

KISS IT!

ABBIE TRAYLER-SMITH

GOST

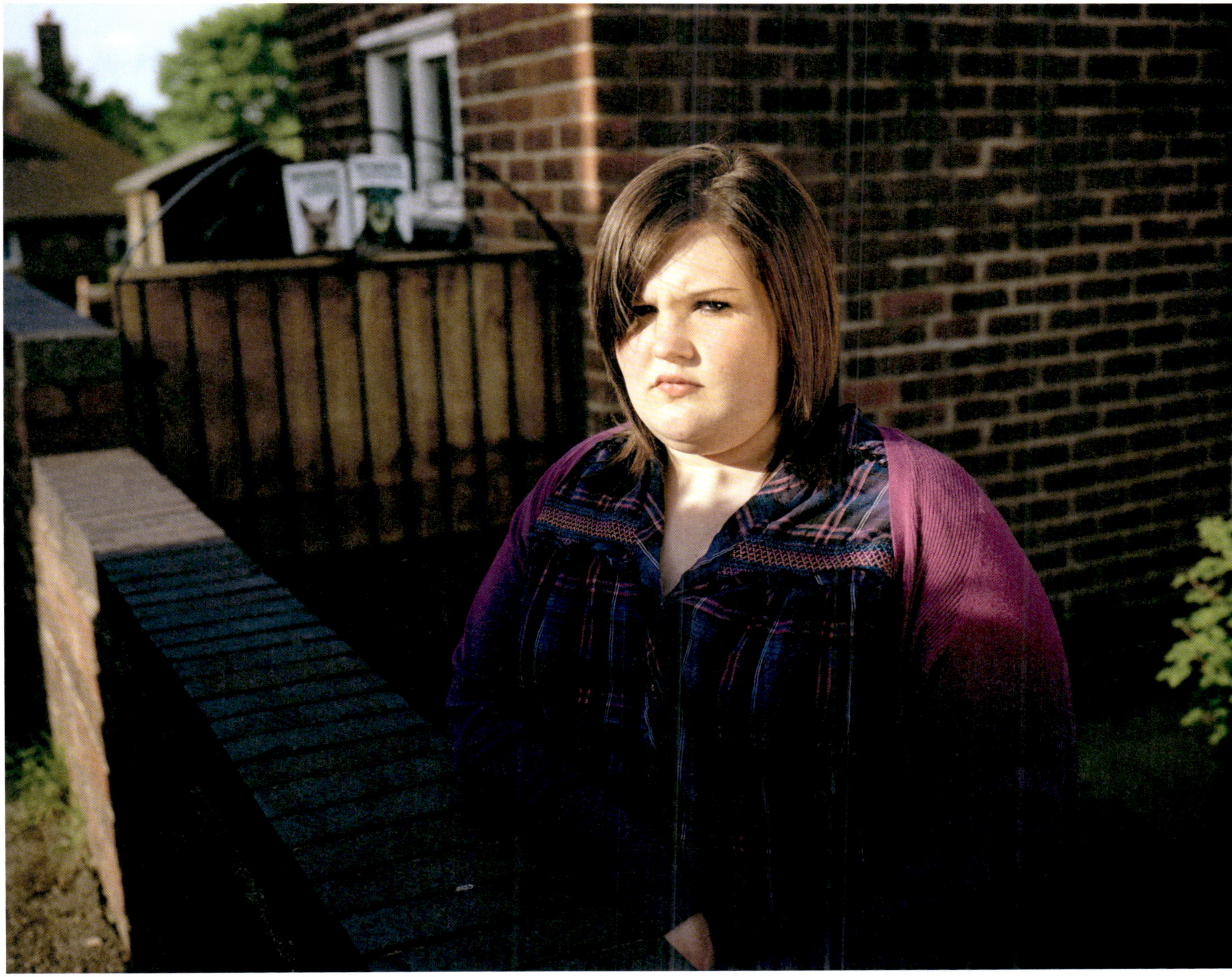

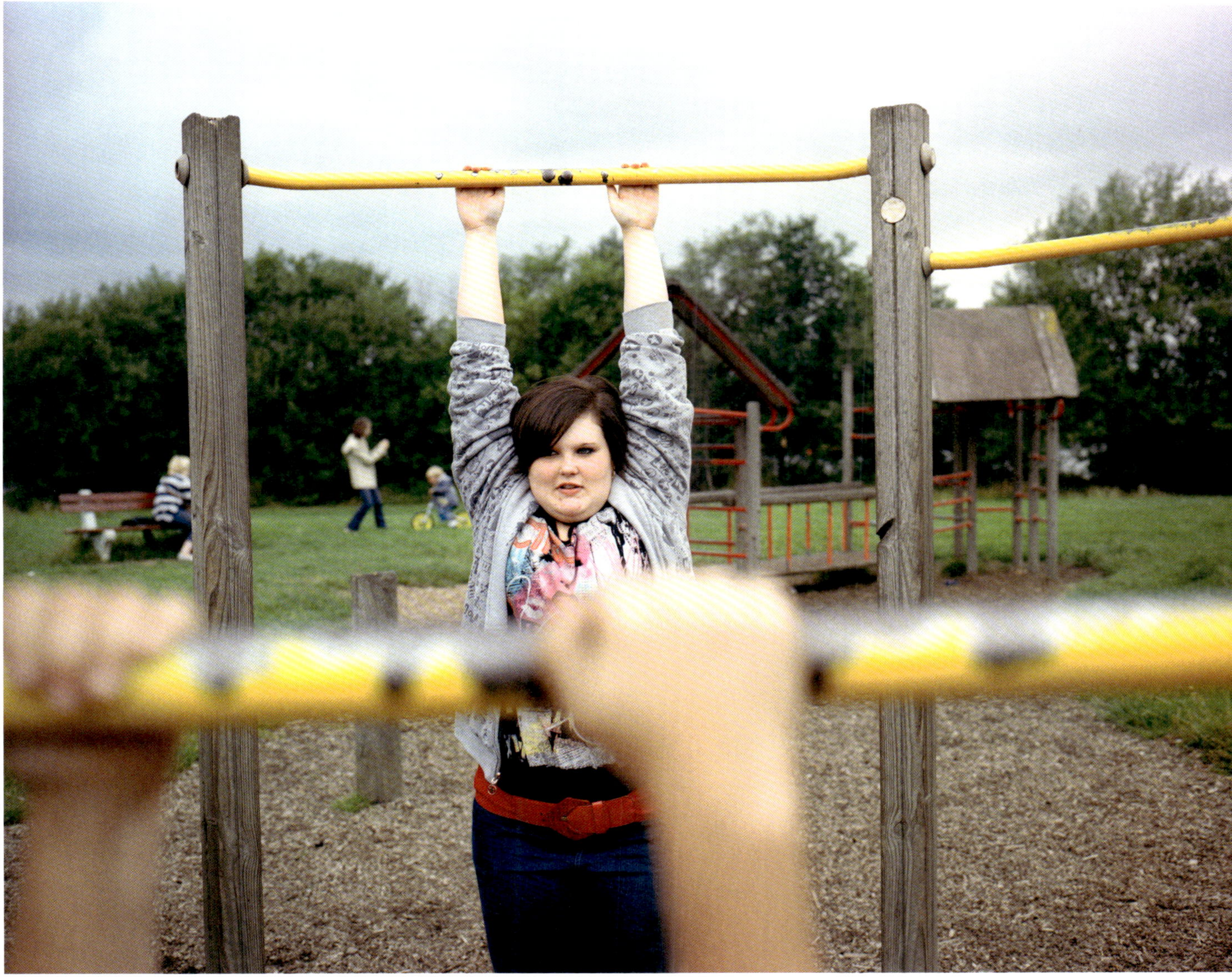

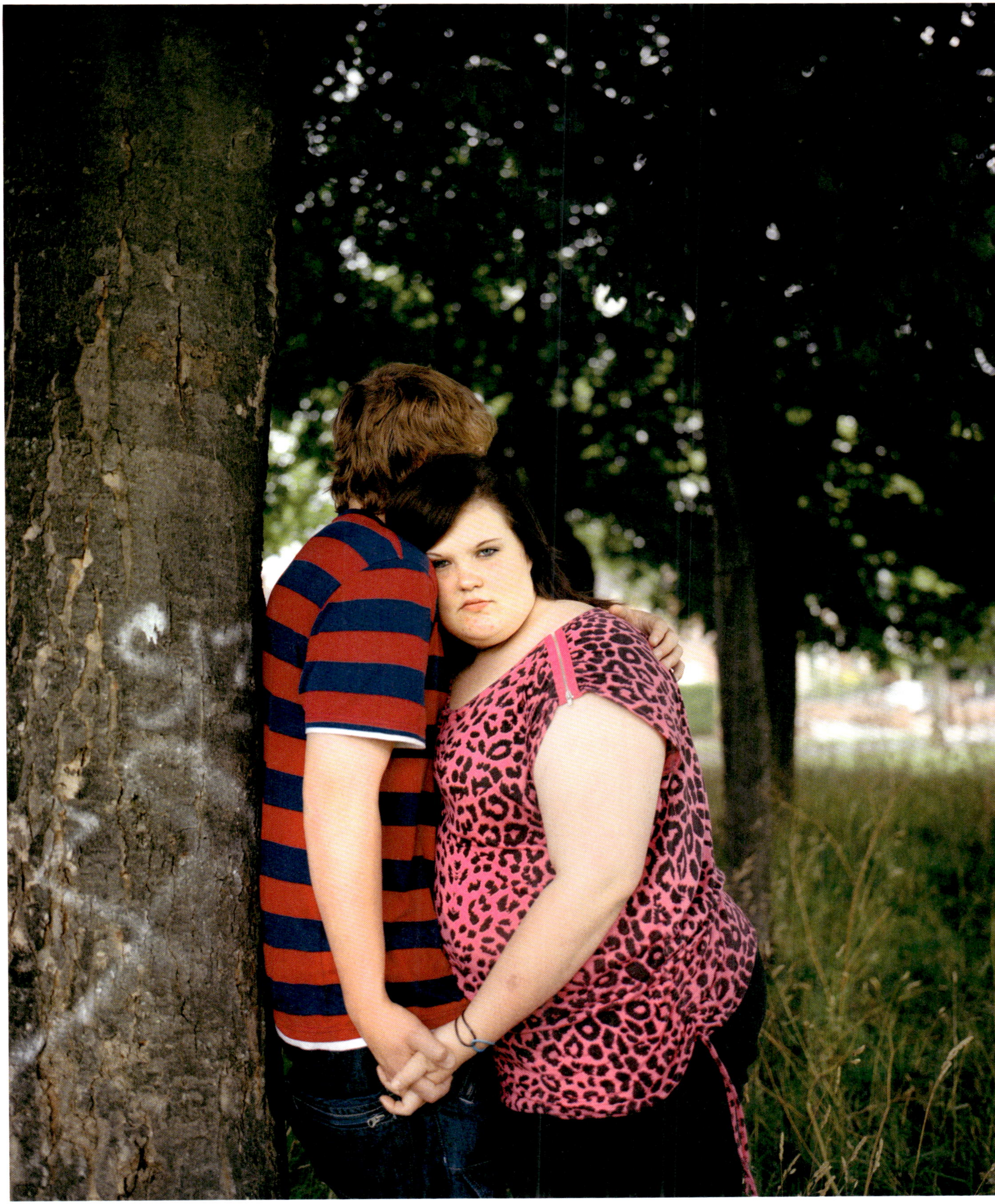

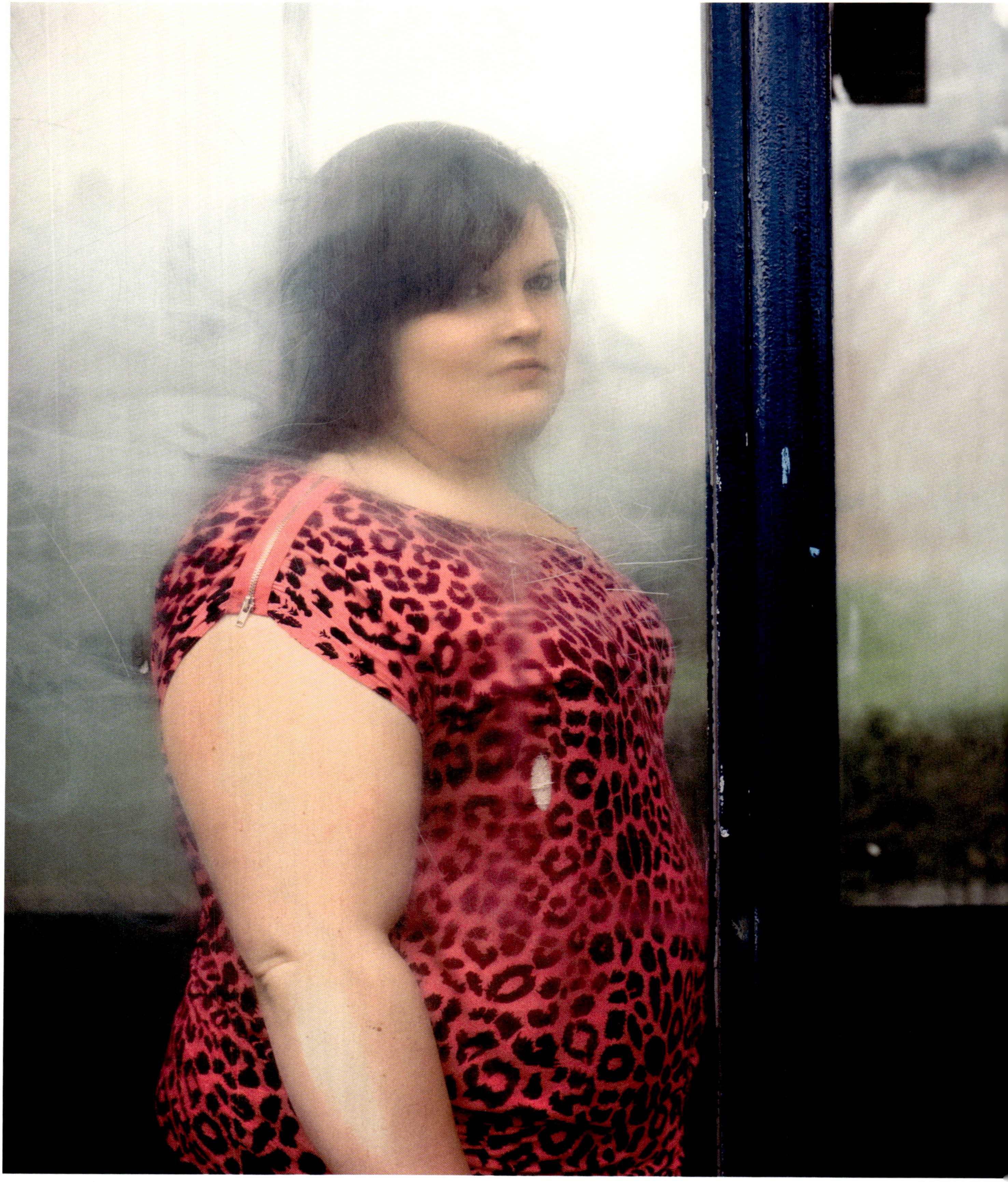

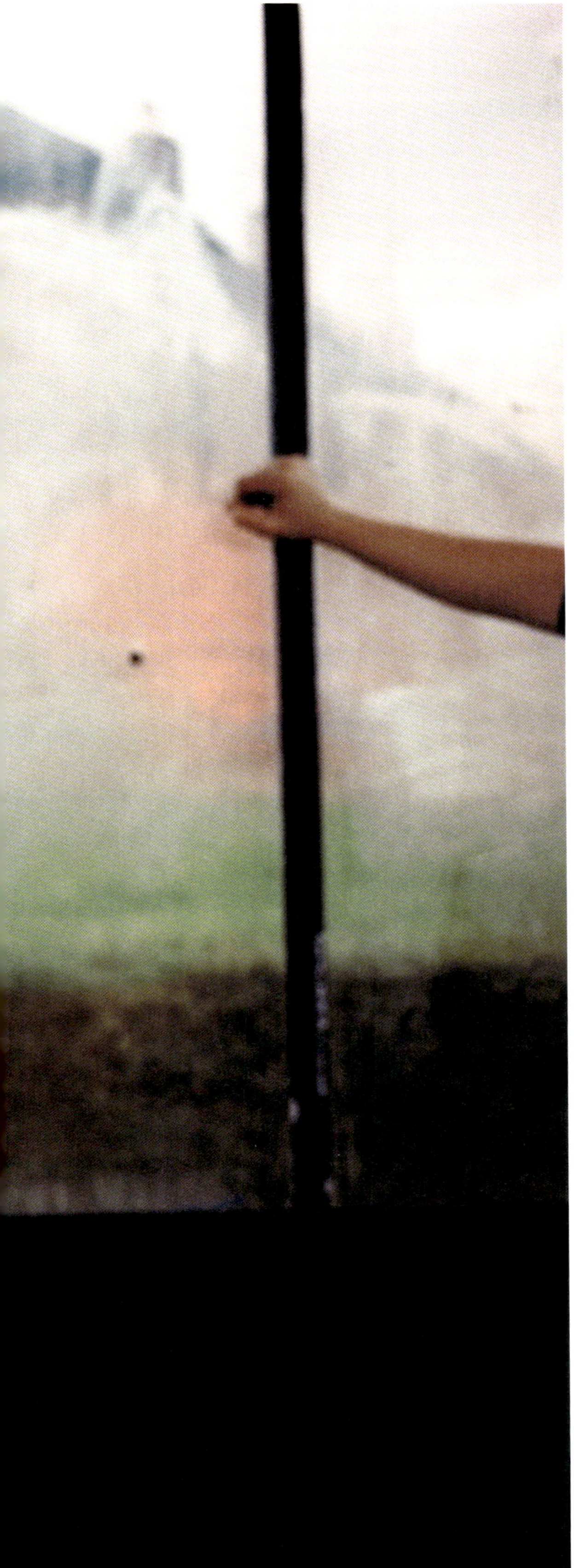

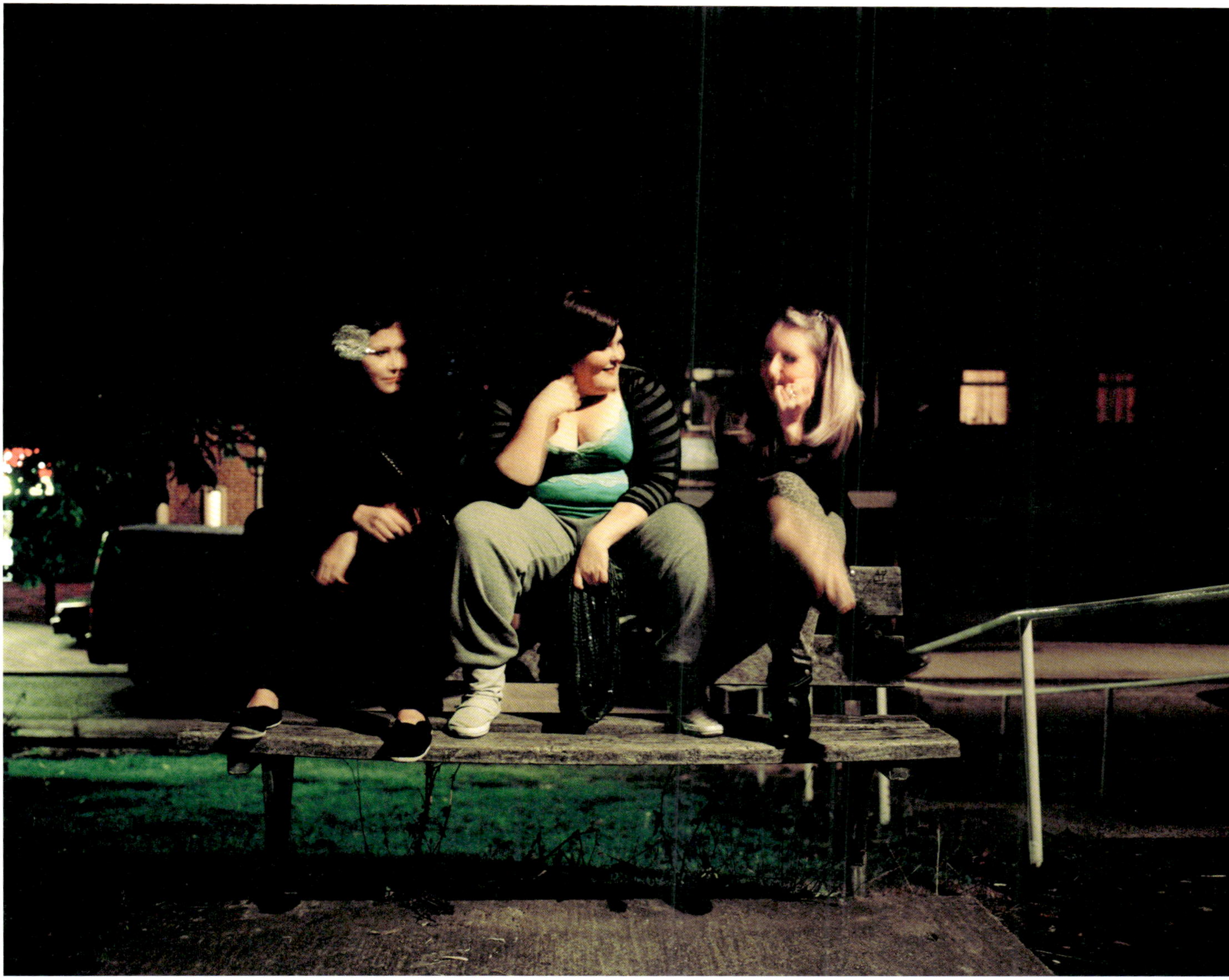

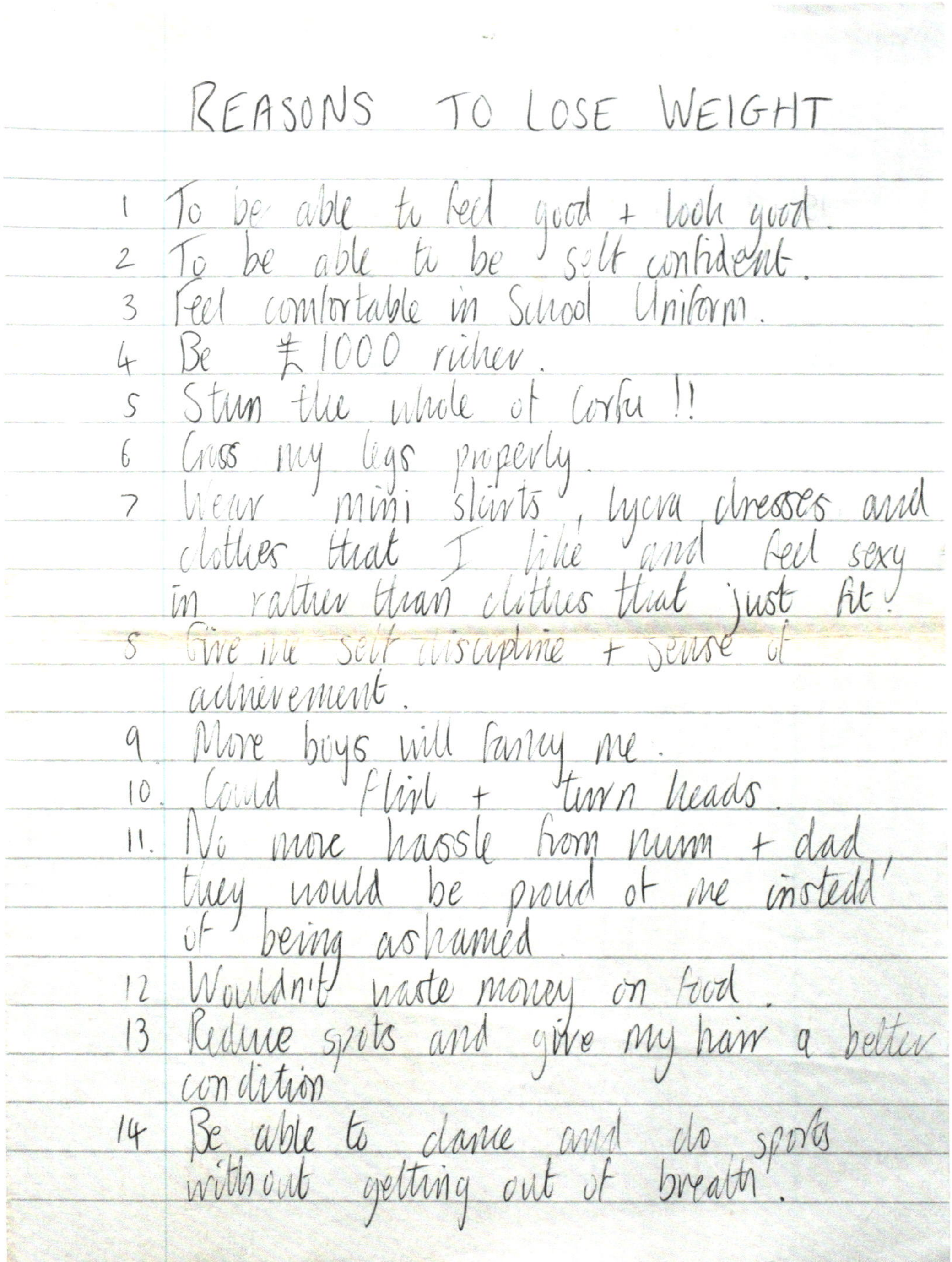

REASONS TO LOSE WEIGHT

1 To be able to feel good + look good.
2 To be able to be self confident.
3 Feel comfortable in School Uniform.
4 Be £1000 richer.
5 Stun the whole of Corfu !!
6 Cross my legs properly.
7 Wear mini skirts, lycra dresses and clothes that I like and feel sexy in rather than clothes that just fit!
8 Give me self discipline + sense of achievement.
9. More boys will fancy me.
10. Could flirt + turn heads.
11. No more hassle from mum + dad, they would be proud of me instead of being ashamed.
12 Wouldn't waste money on food.
13 Reduce spots and give my hair a better condition
14 Be able to dance and do sports without getting out of breath.

A list of reasons to lose weight, written by Abbie. Age 15, 1992

15 I would have a better chance in life ie I wouldn't be predjudiced against about being fat.

16 Could really be my own true person and have the freedom to do what the hell I like.

17 BE ONE THOUSAND POUNDS RICHER !!

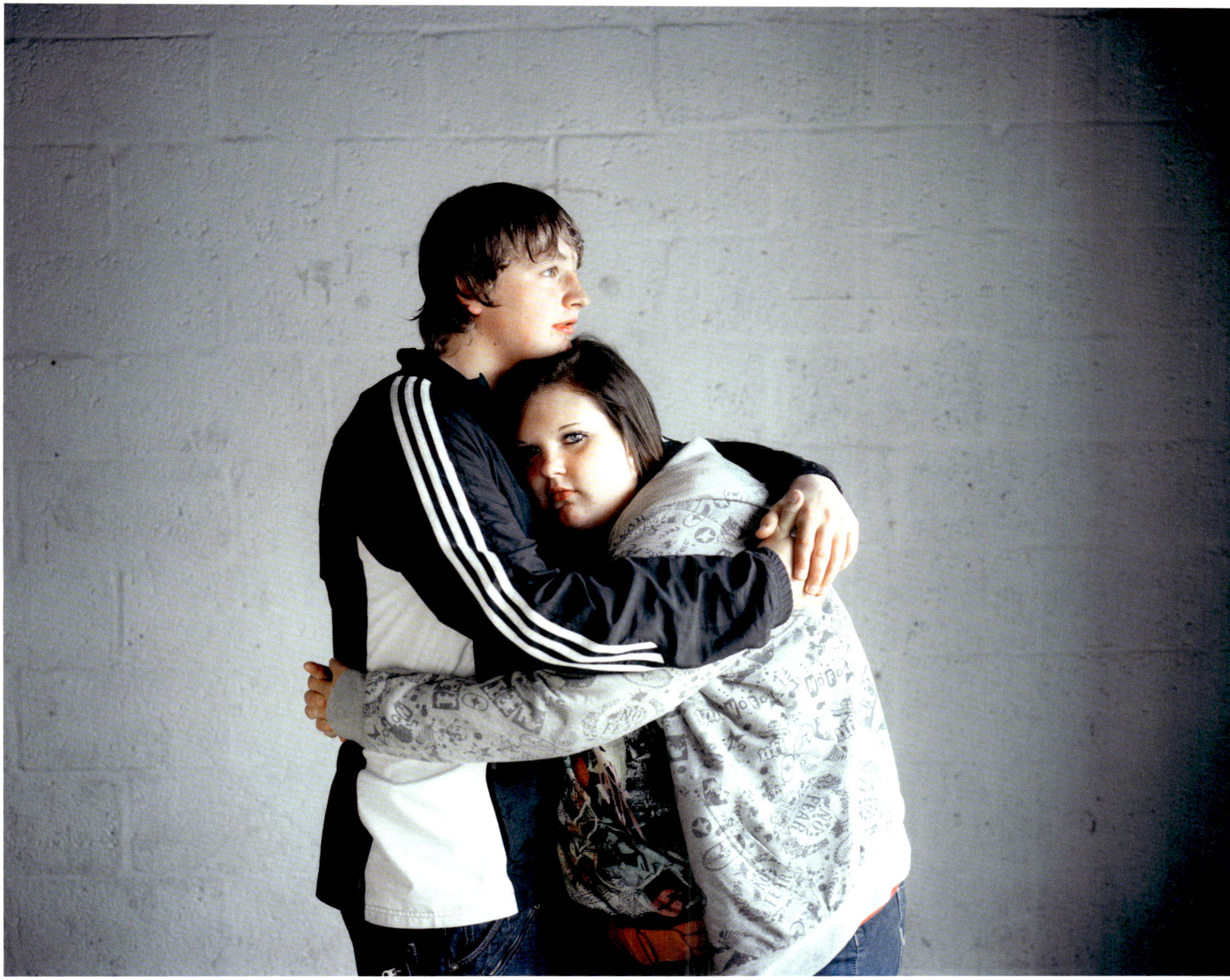

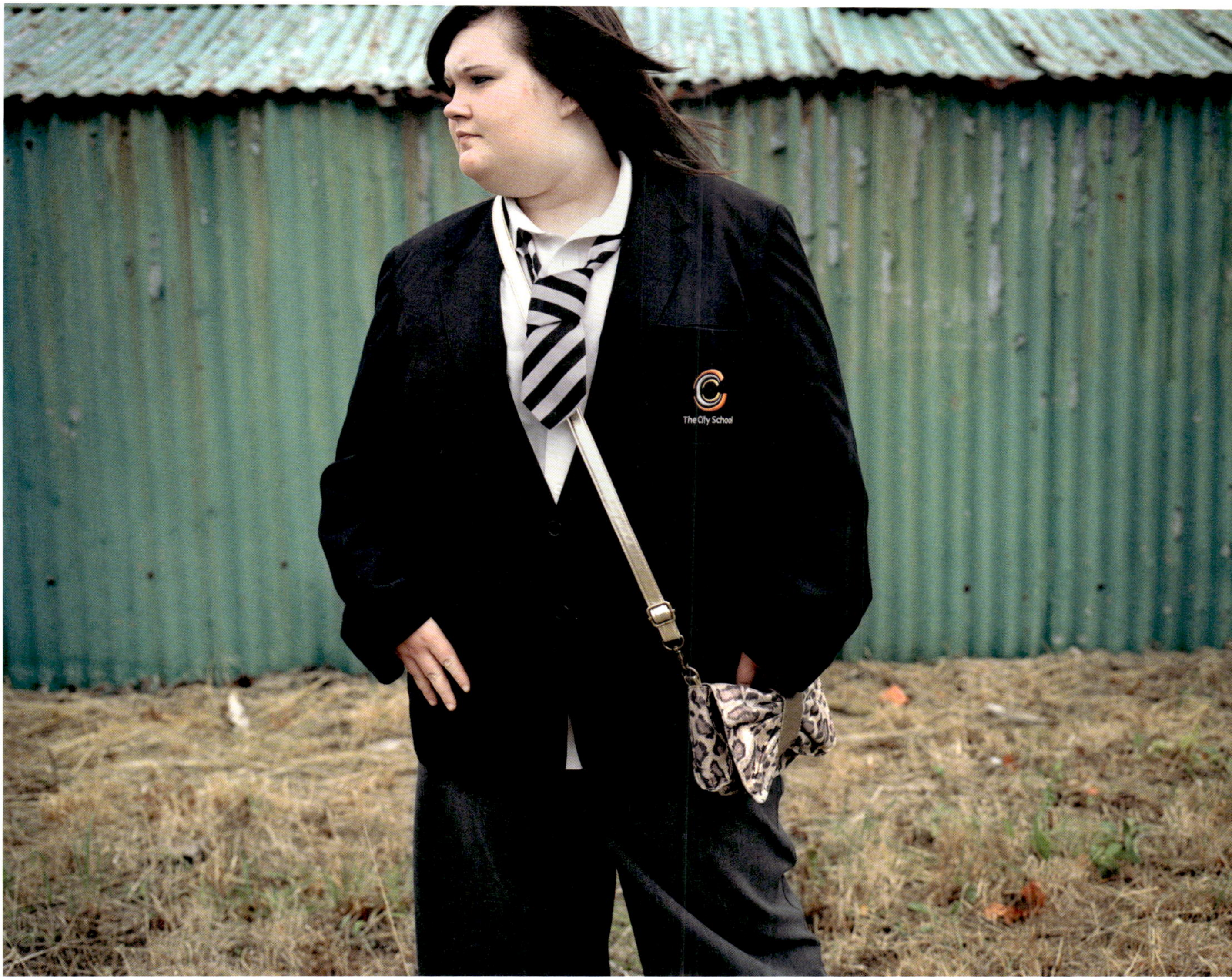
The City School

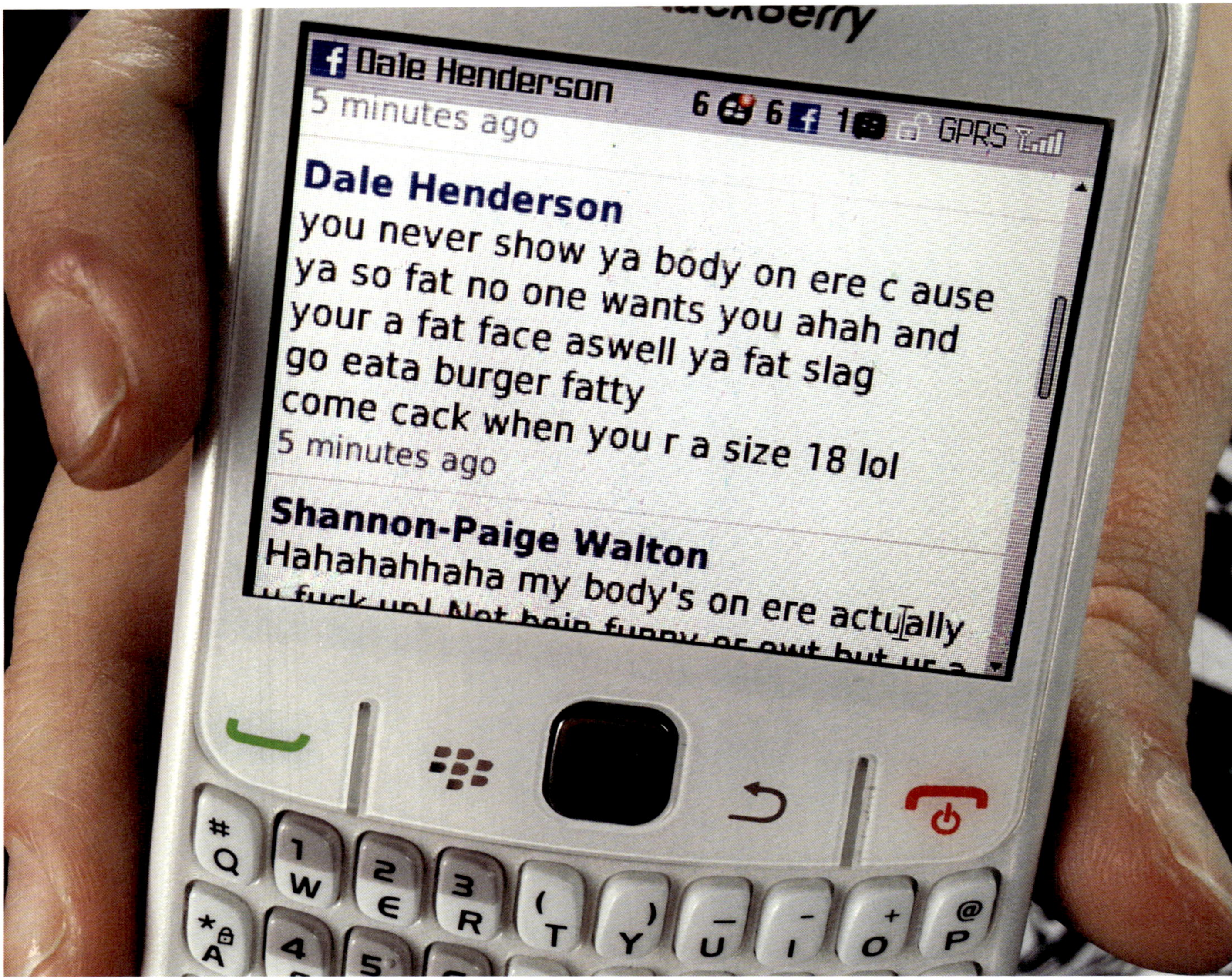
Dale Henderson
5 minutes ago
Dale Henderson
you never show ya body on ere c ause
ya so fat no one wants you ahah and
your a fat face aswell ya fat slag
go eata burger fatty
come cack when you r a size 18 lol
5 minutes ago
Shannon-Paige Walton
Hahahahhhaha my body's on ere actually

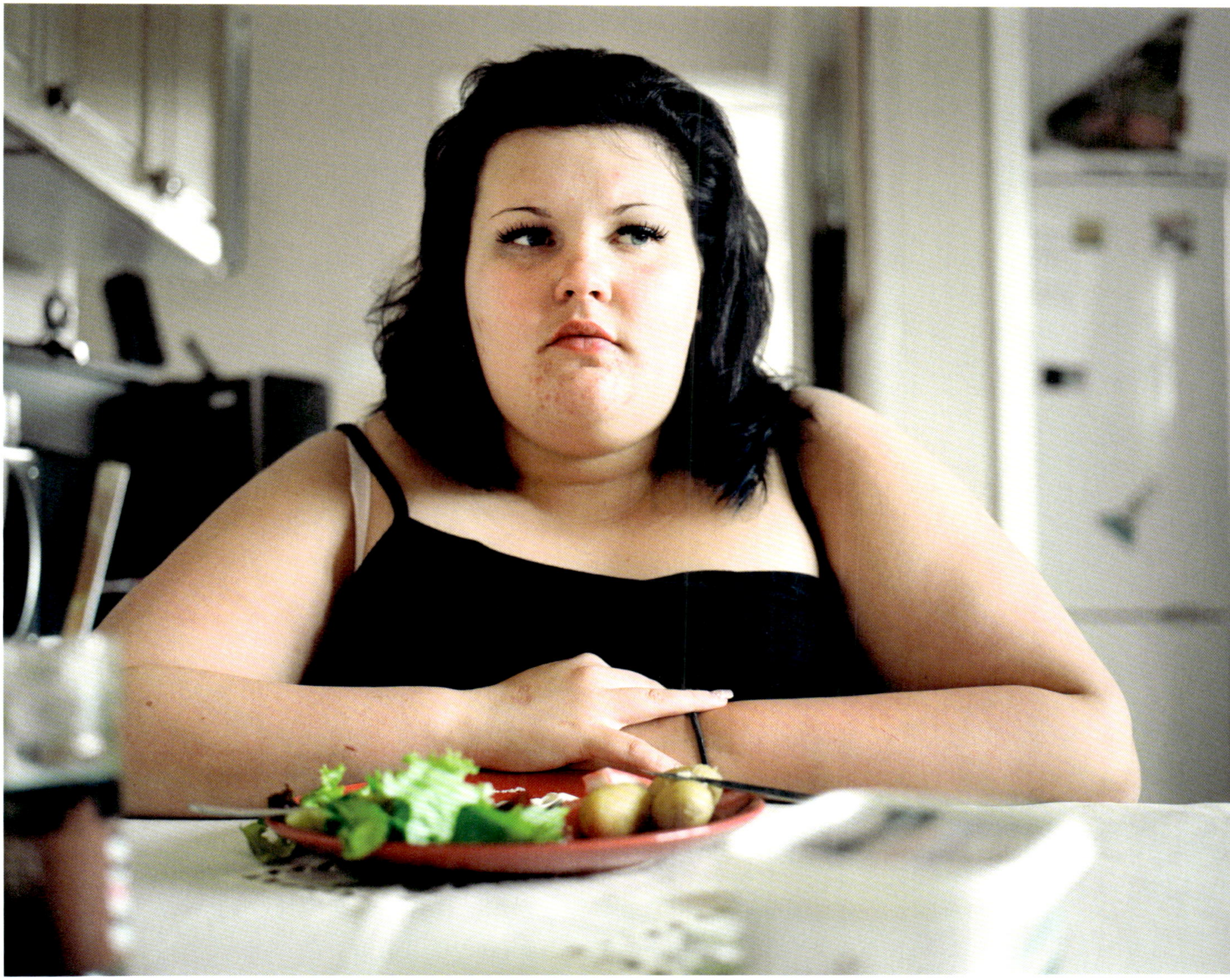

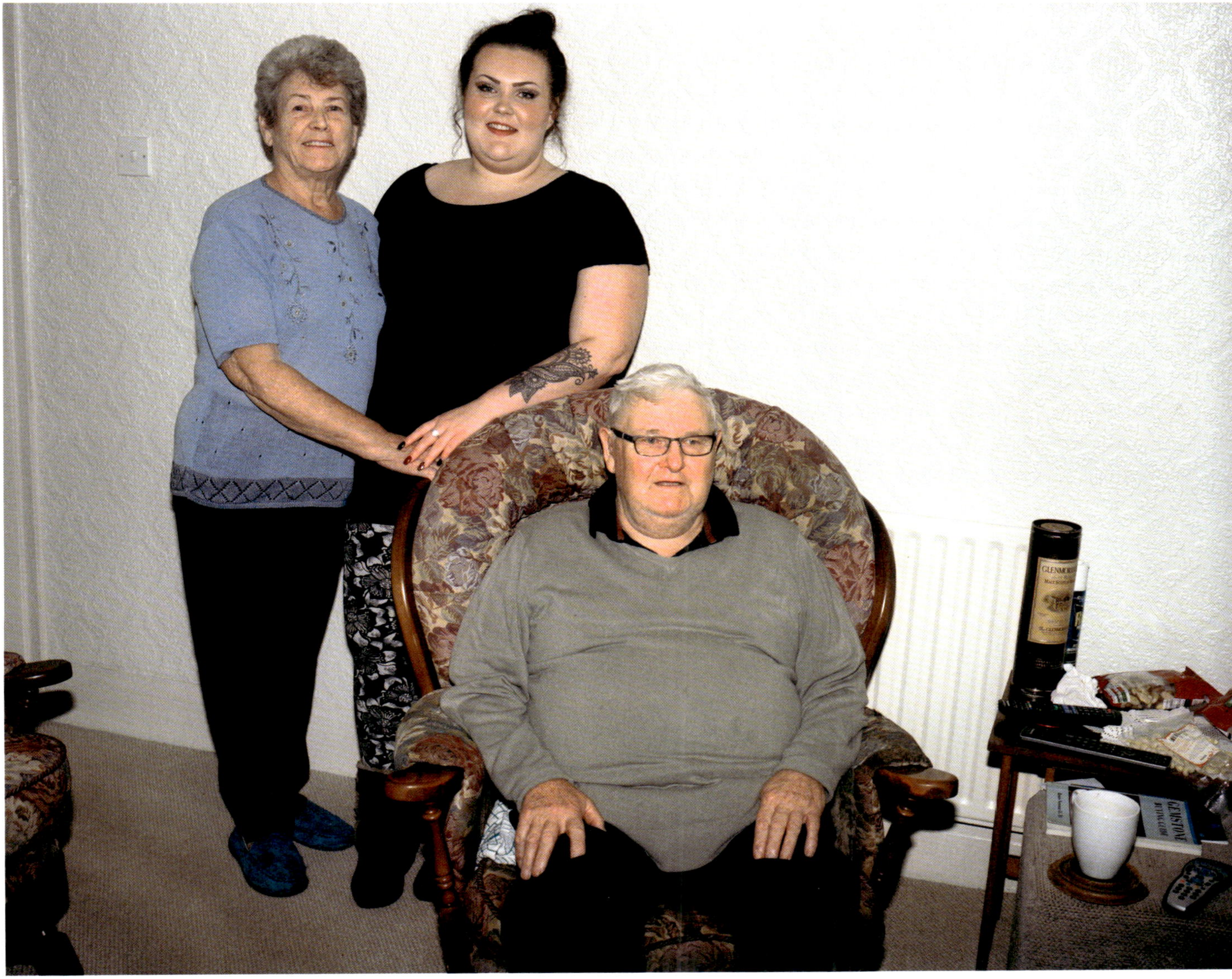

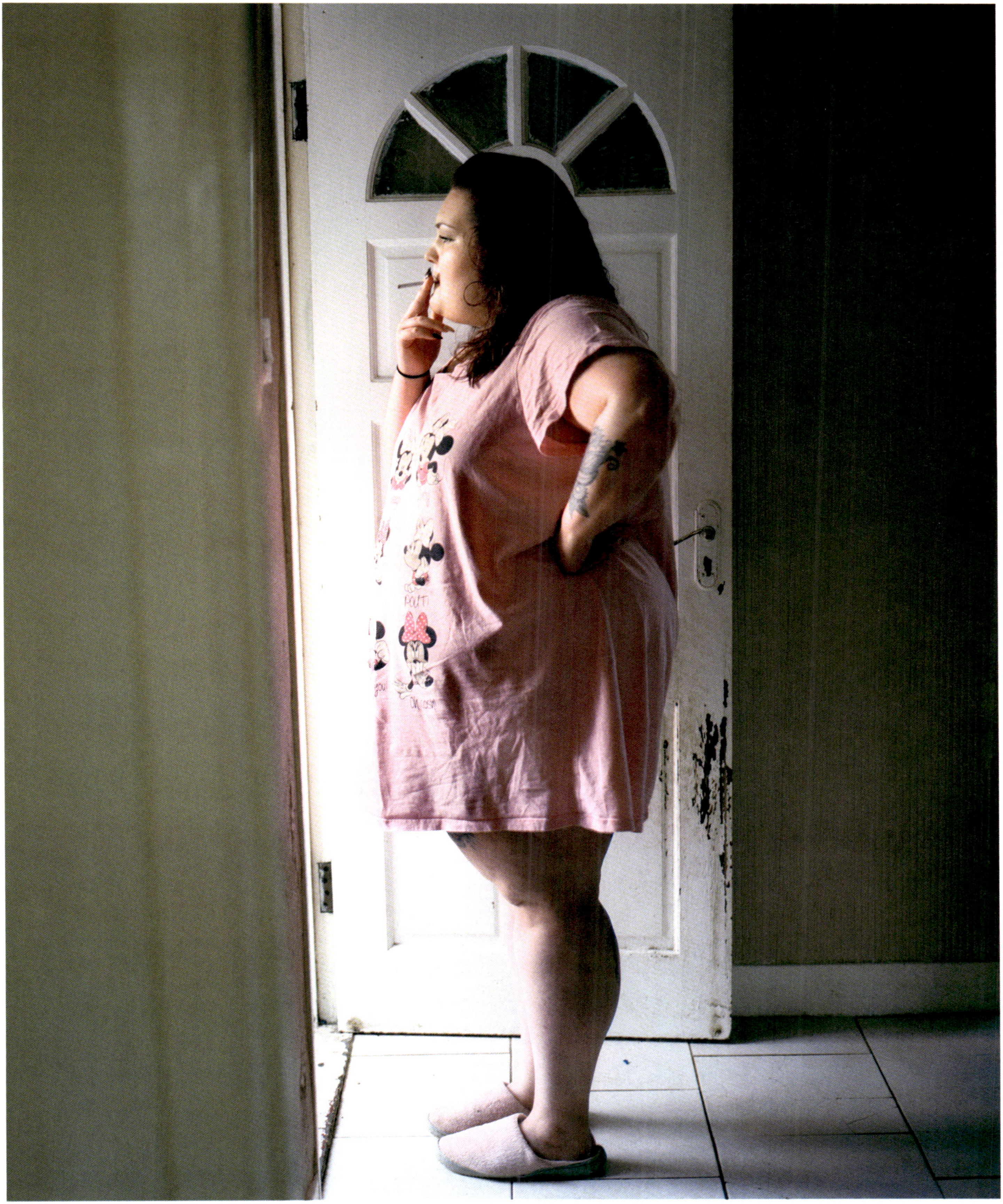

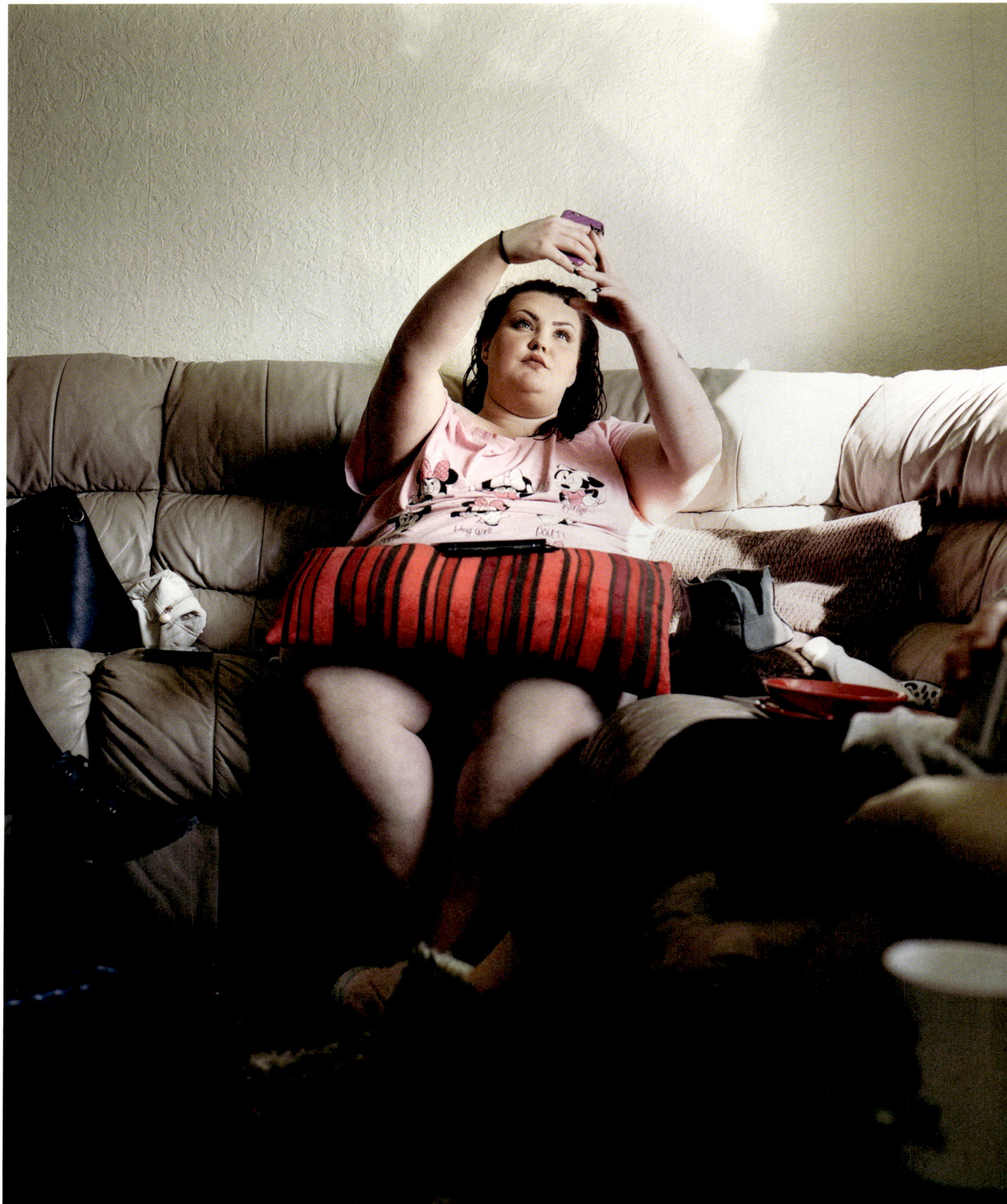

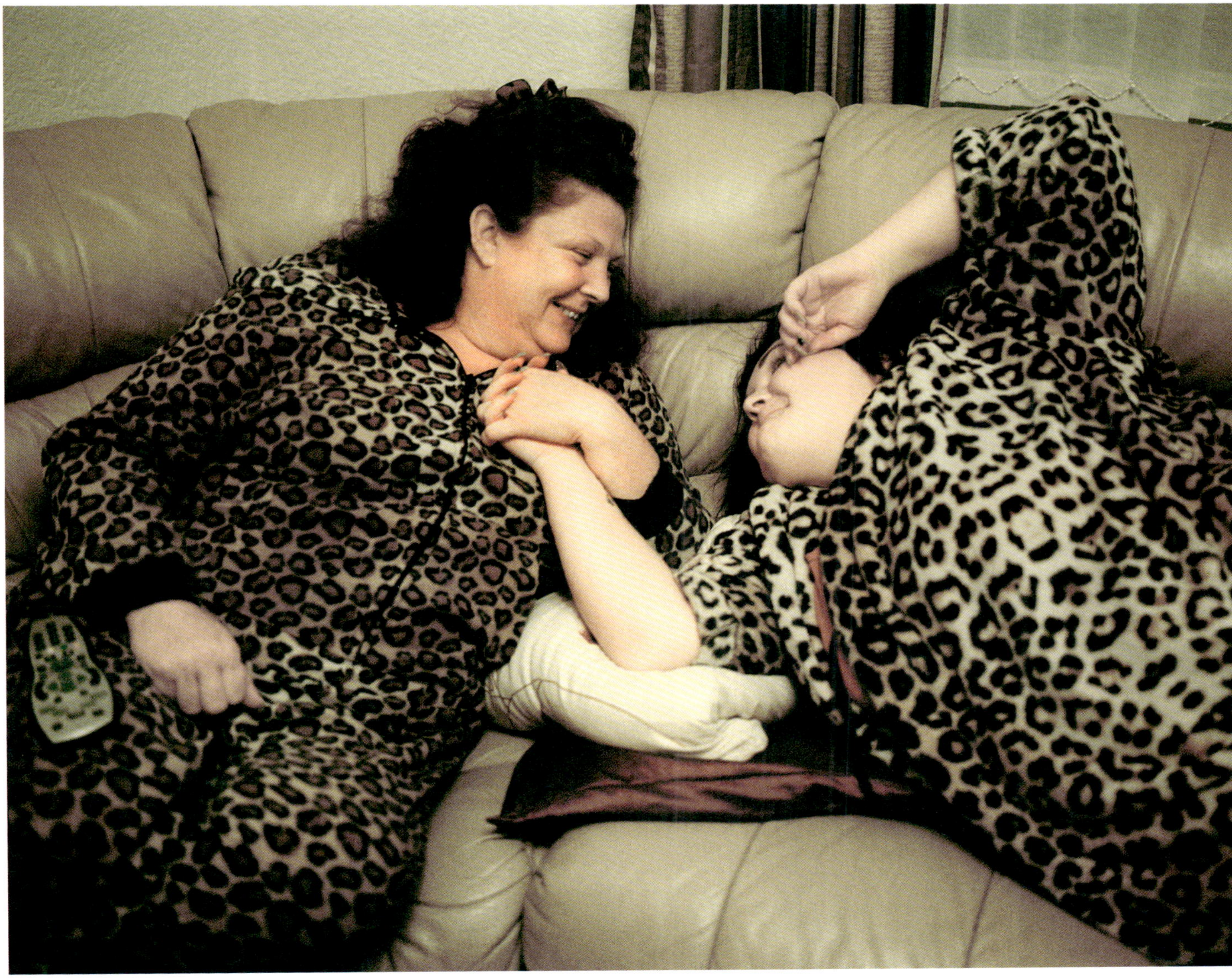

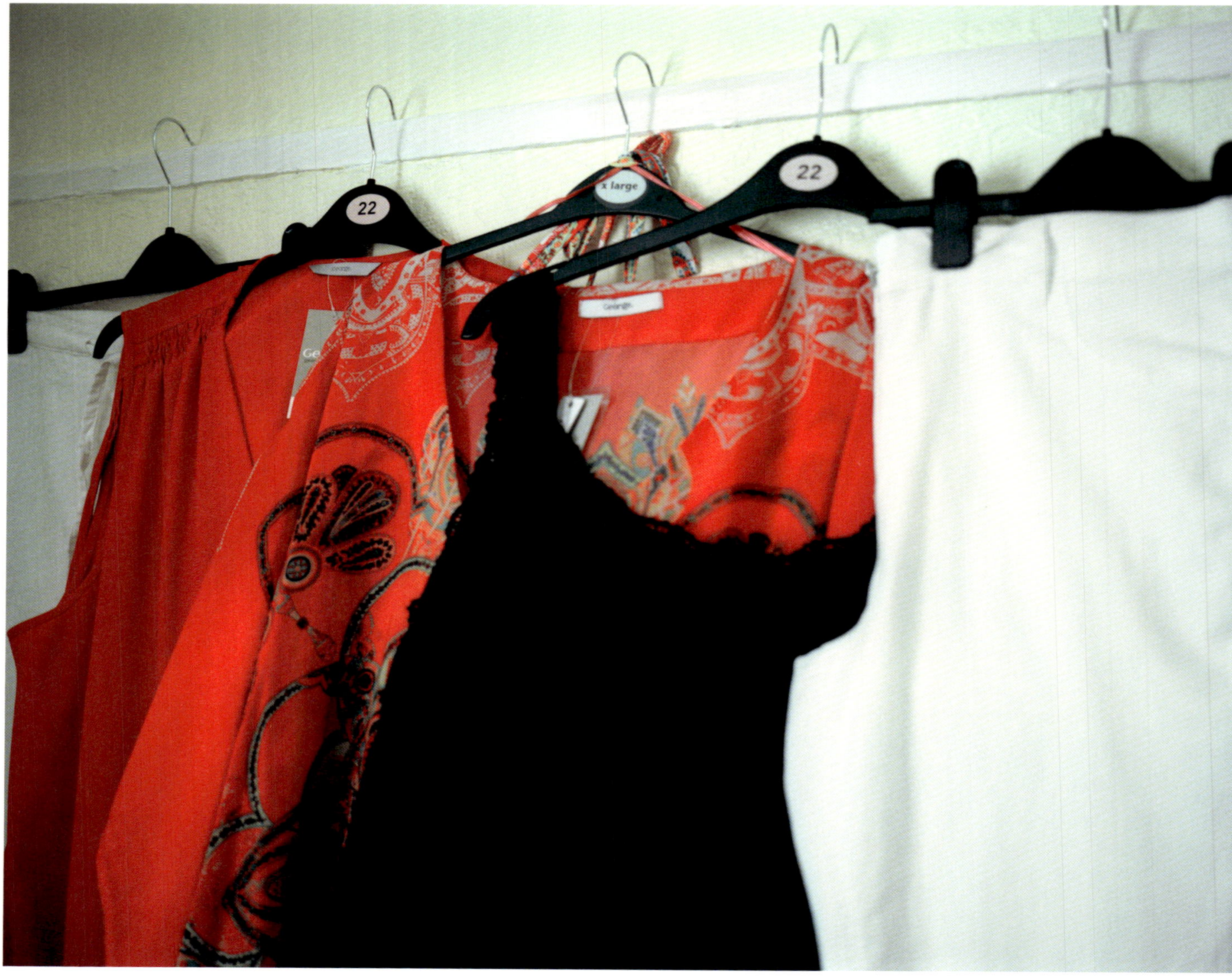
22
x large
22

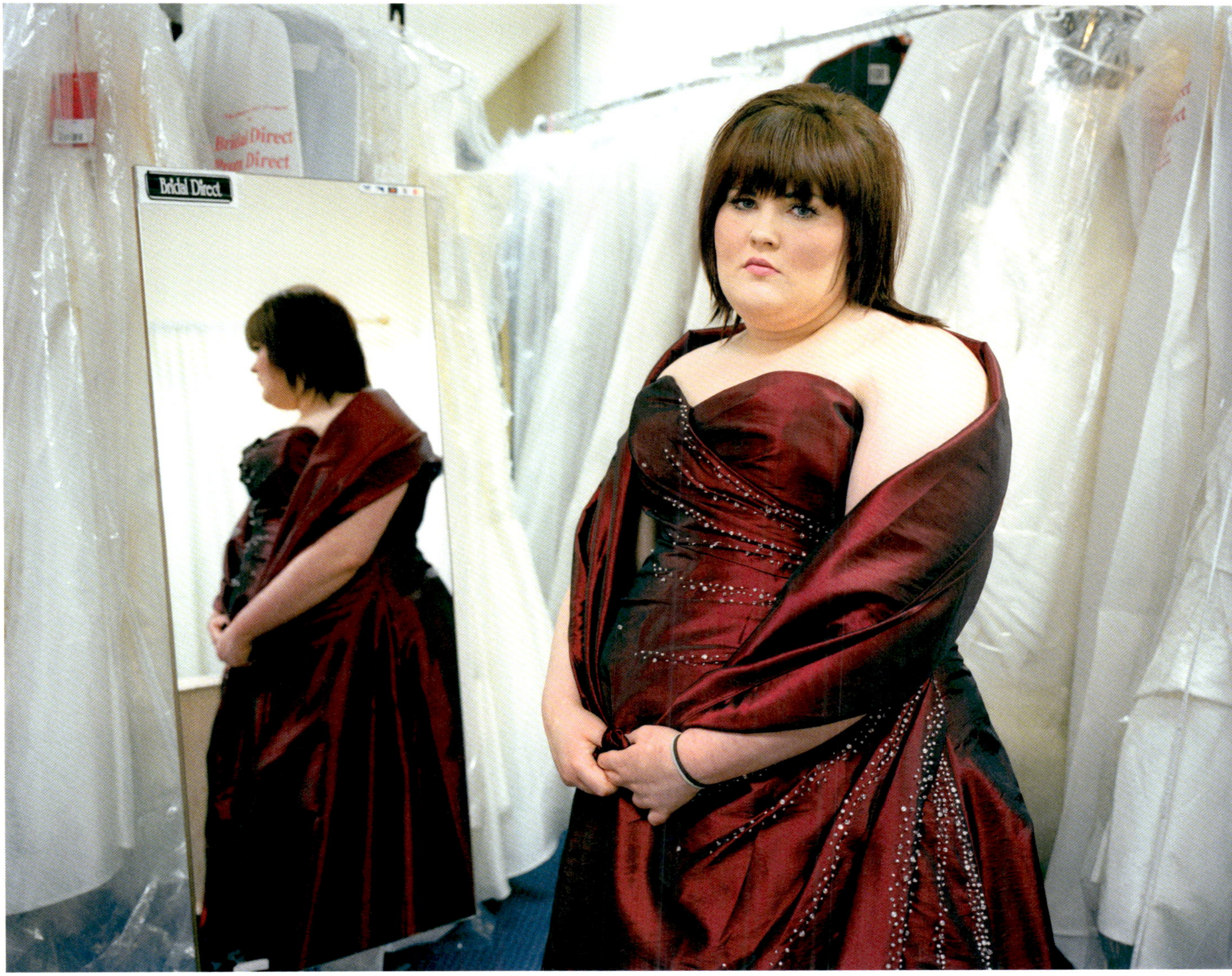
Bridal Direct
Bridal Direct

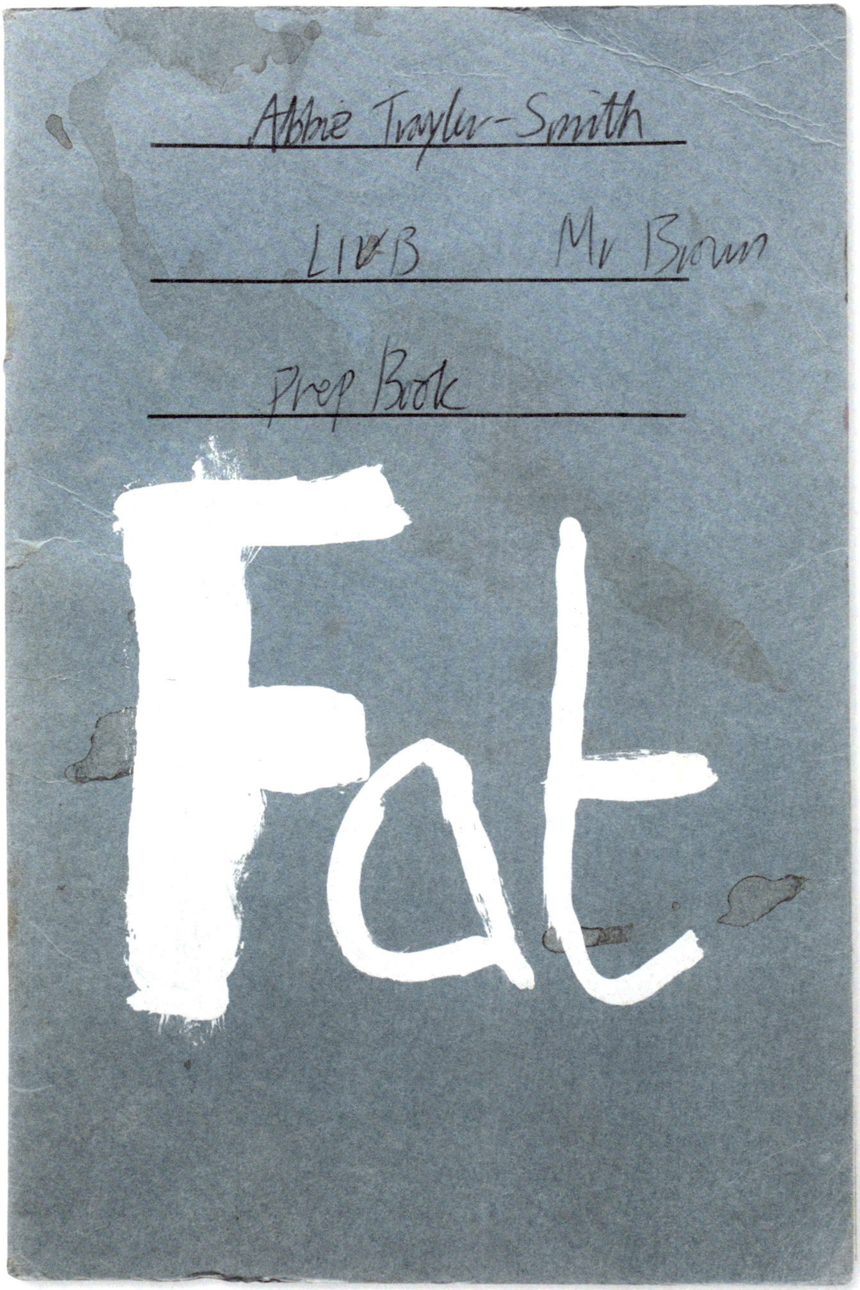

The word 'FAT' typex'd on the front of Abbie's schoolbook to remind herself to stick to her diet. Age 14, 1991

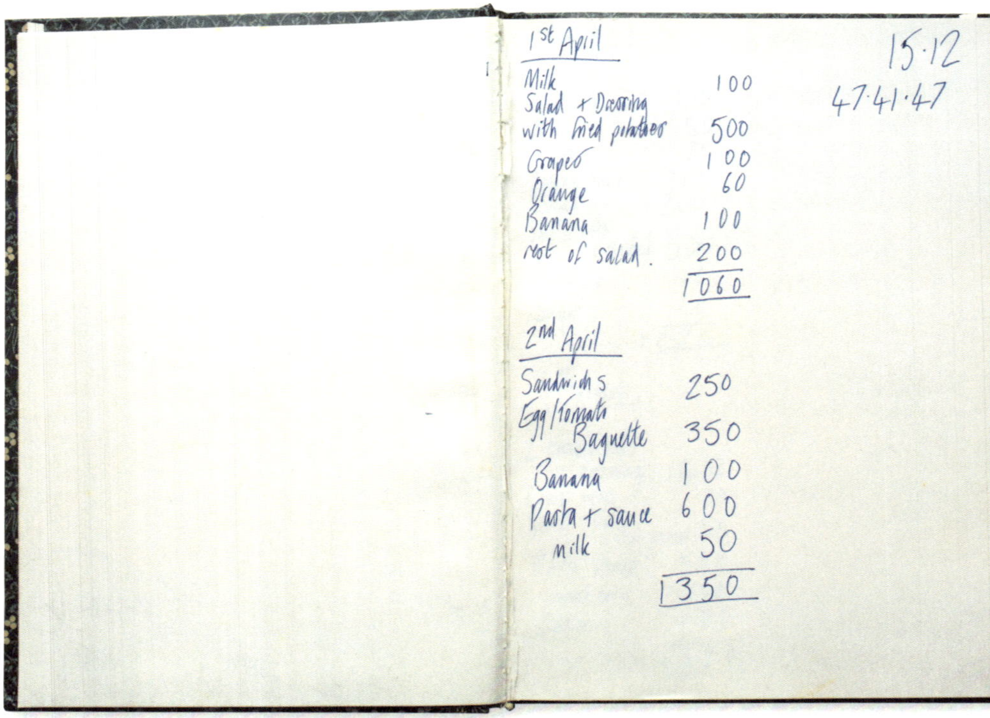

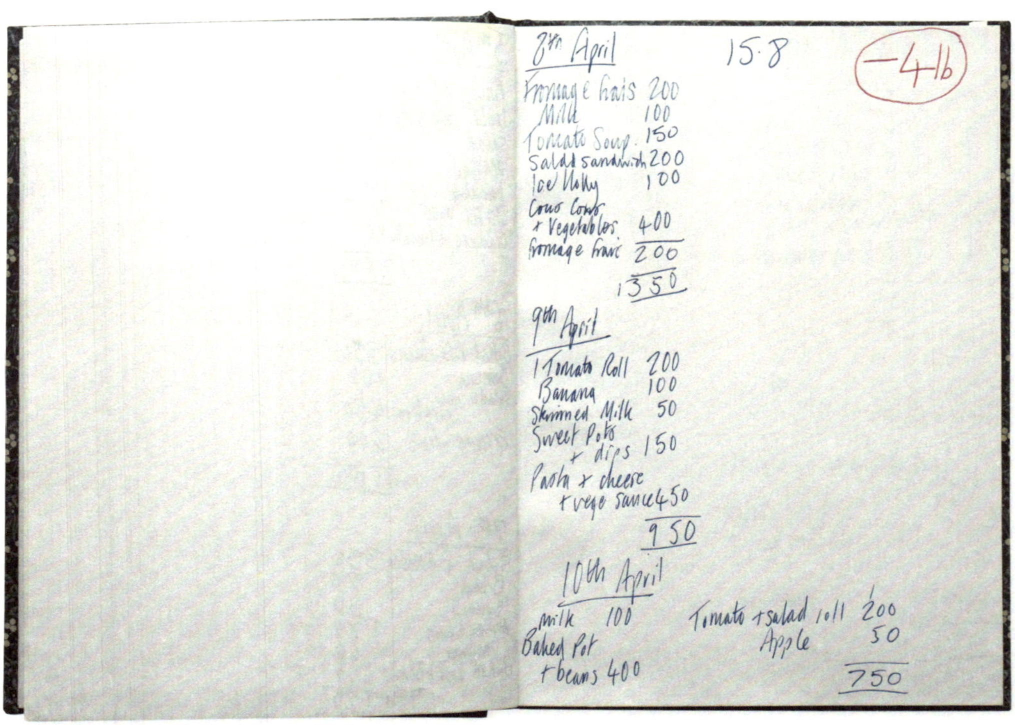

One of Abbie's 'diet diaries' used to record her daily food intake, calories, weight and measurements. The diaries were usually completed for a few weeks before the pages became blank again. Age 14, 1991

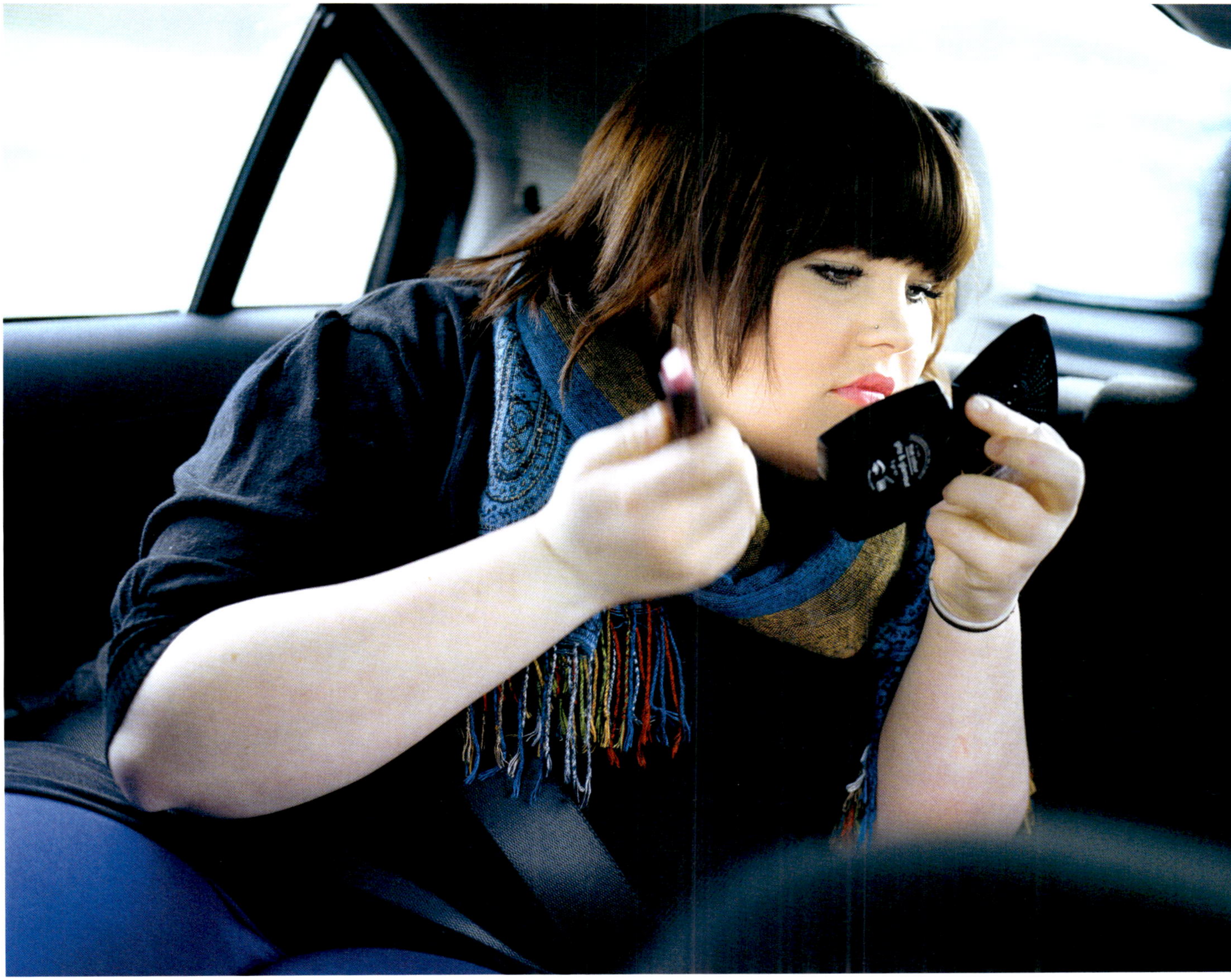

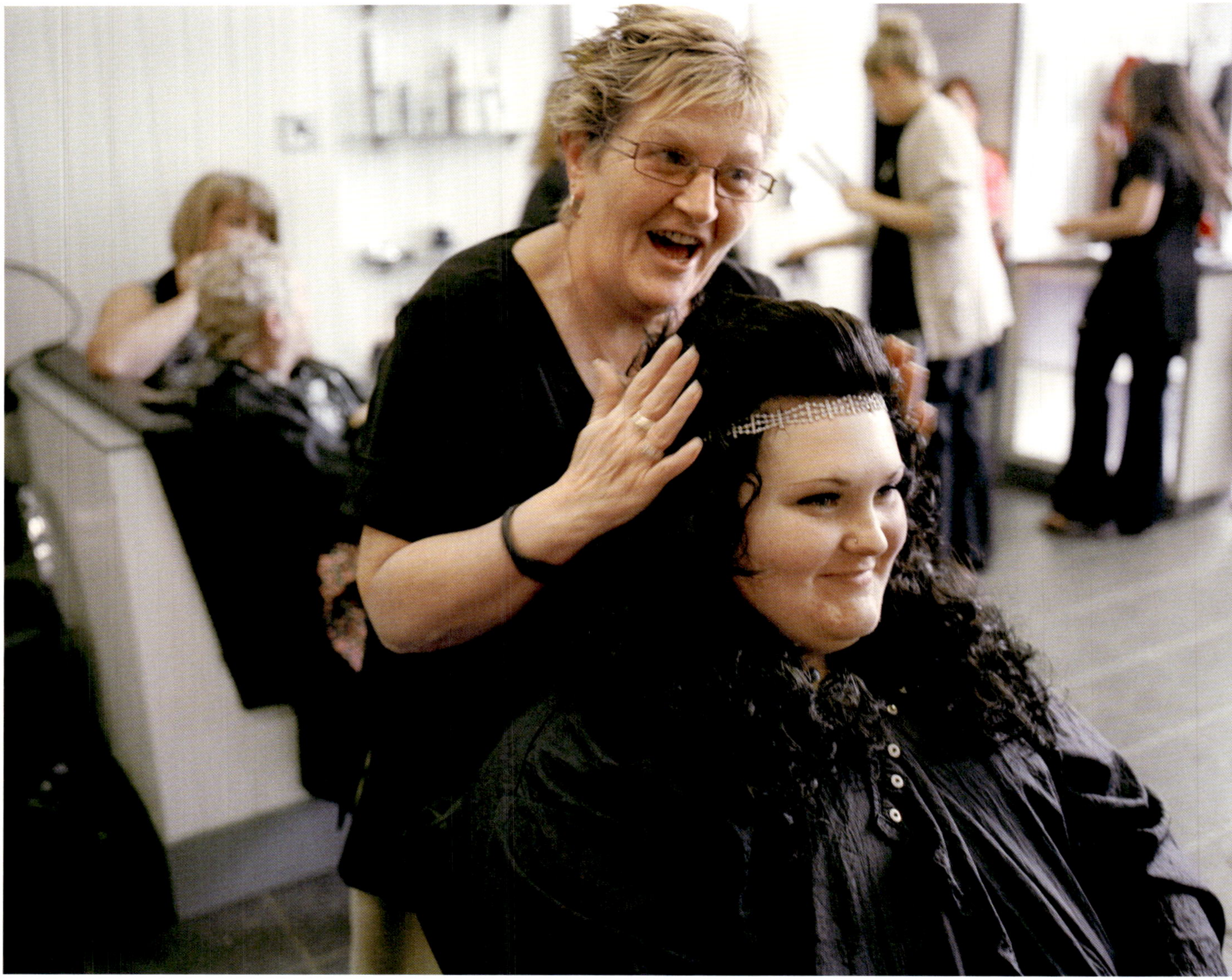

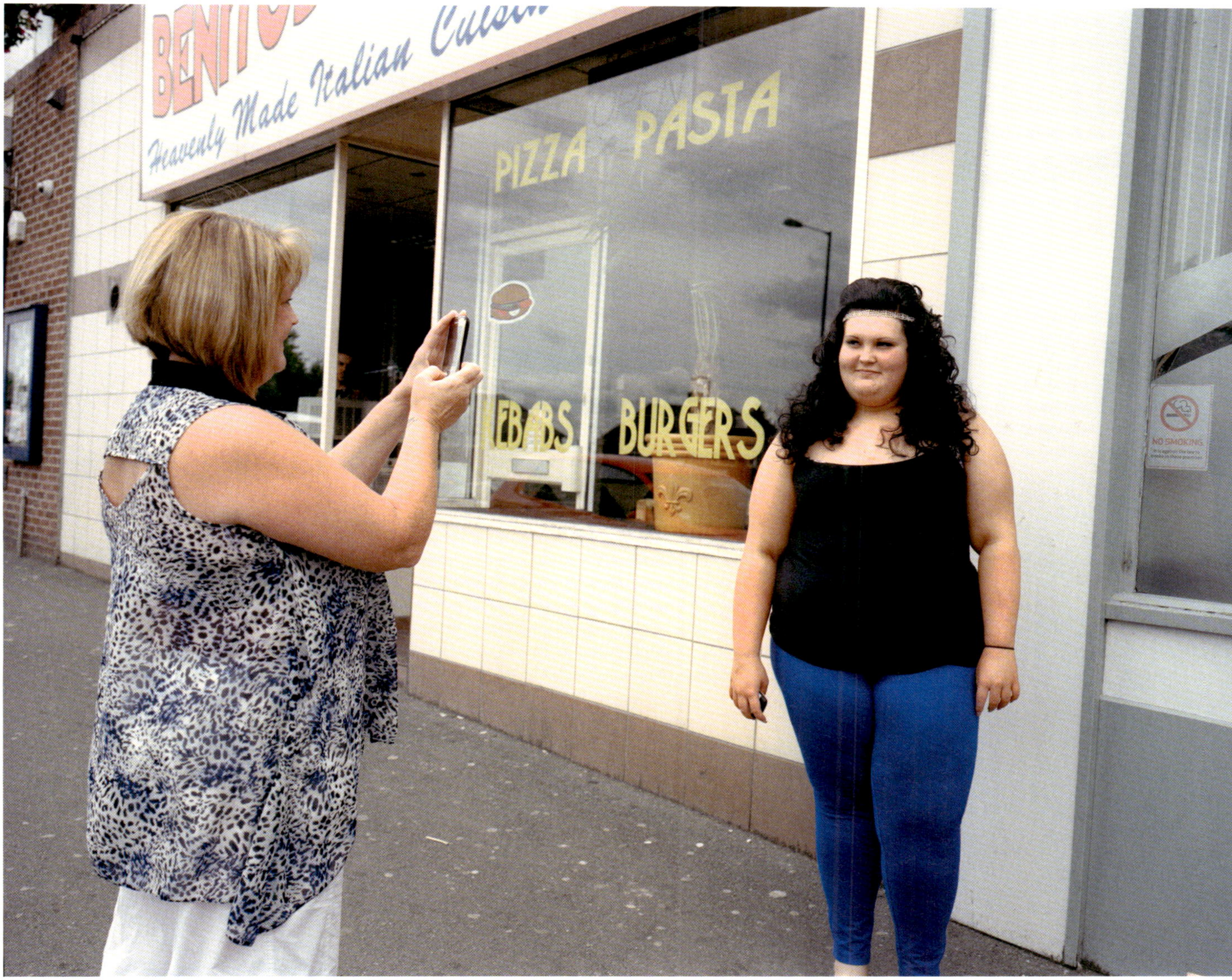
Heavenly Made Italian
PIZZA PASTA
BURGERS
NO SMOKING

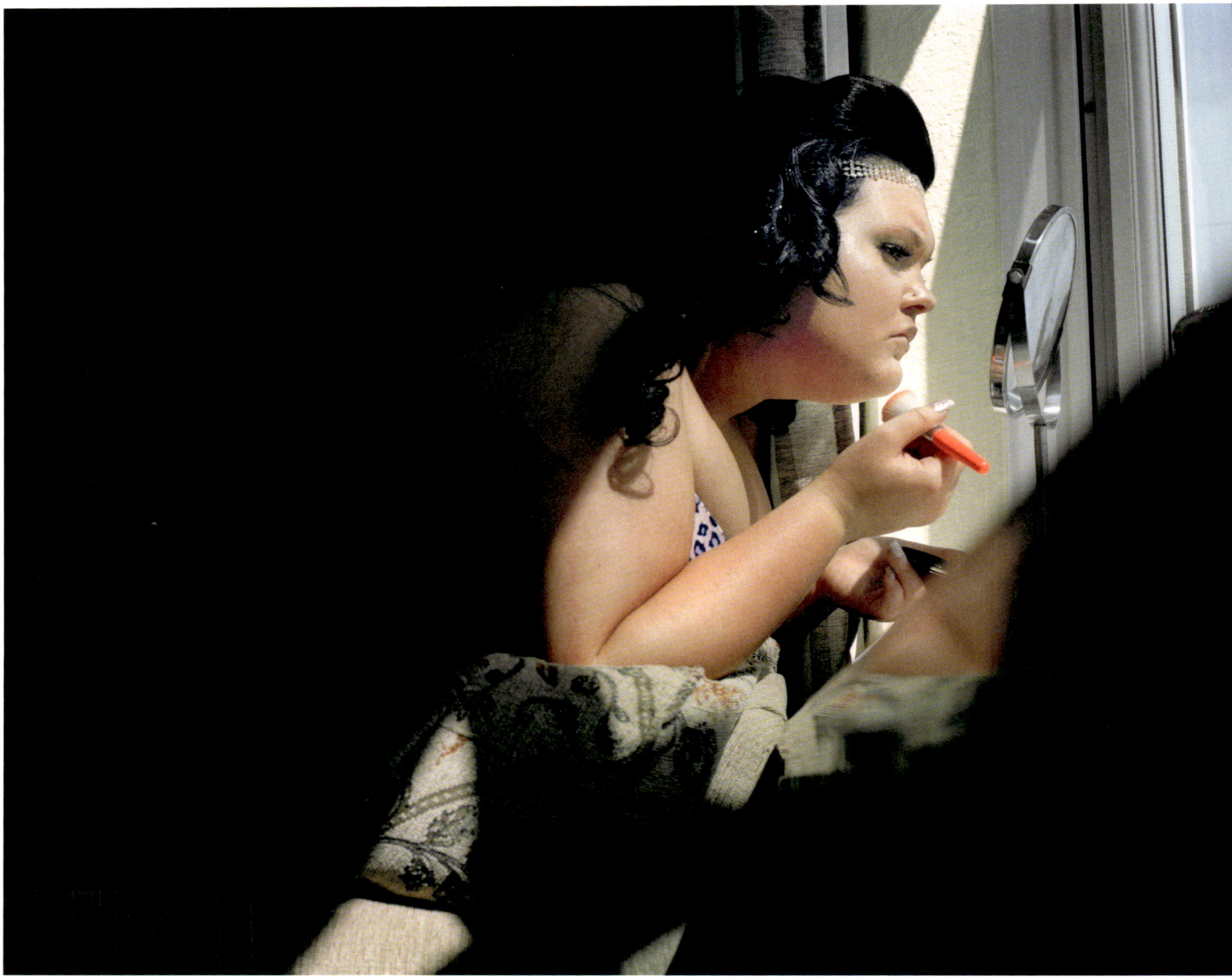

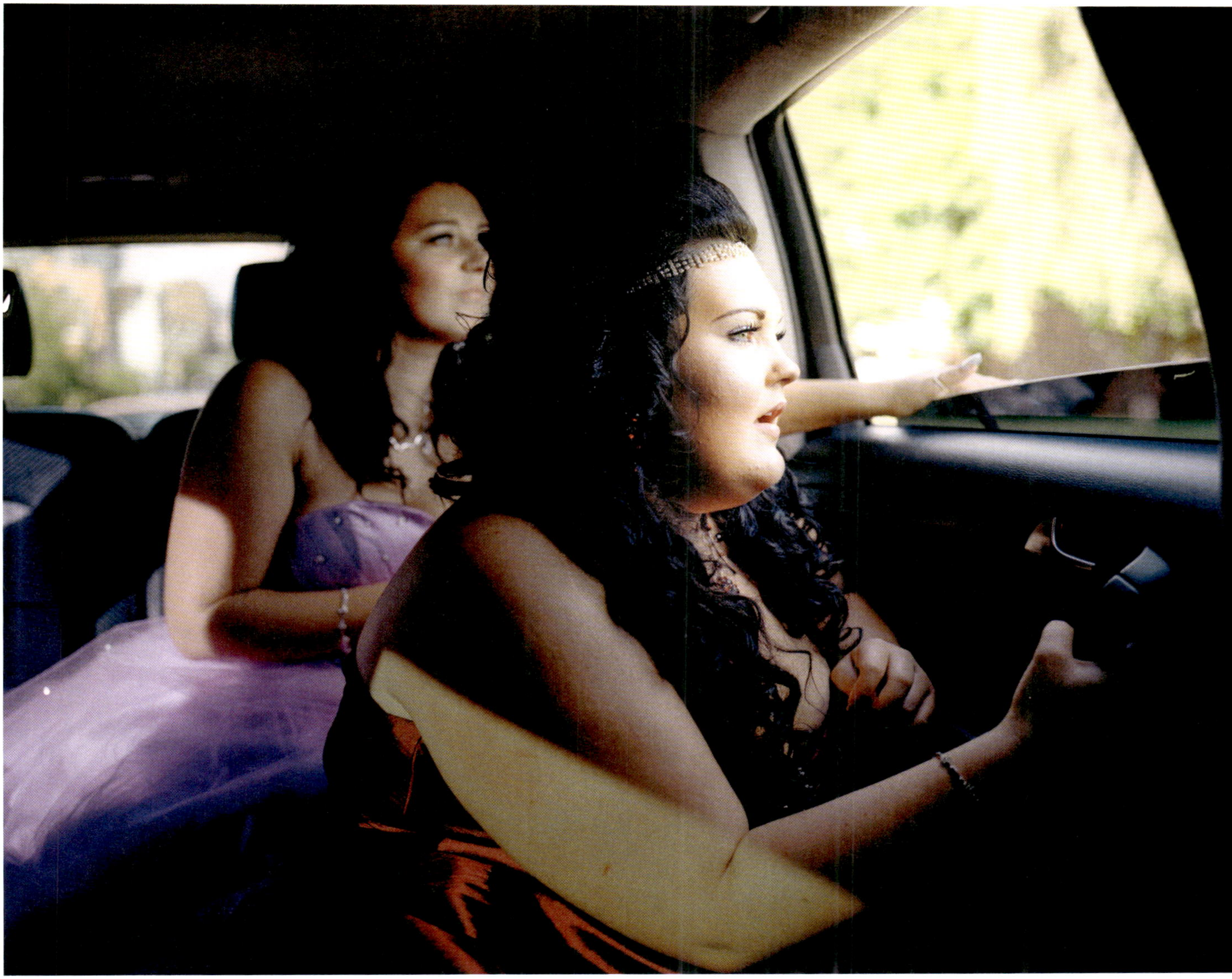

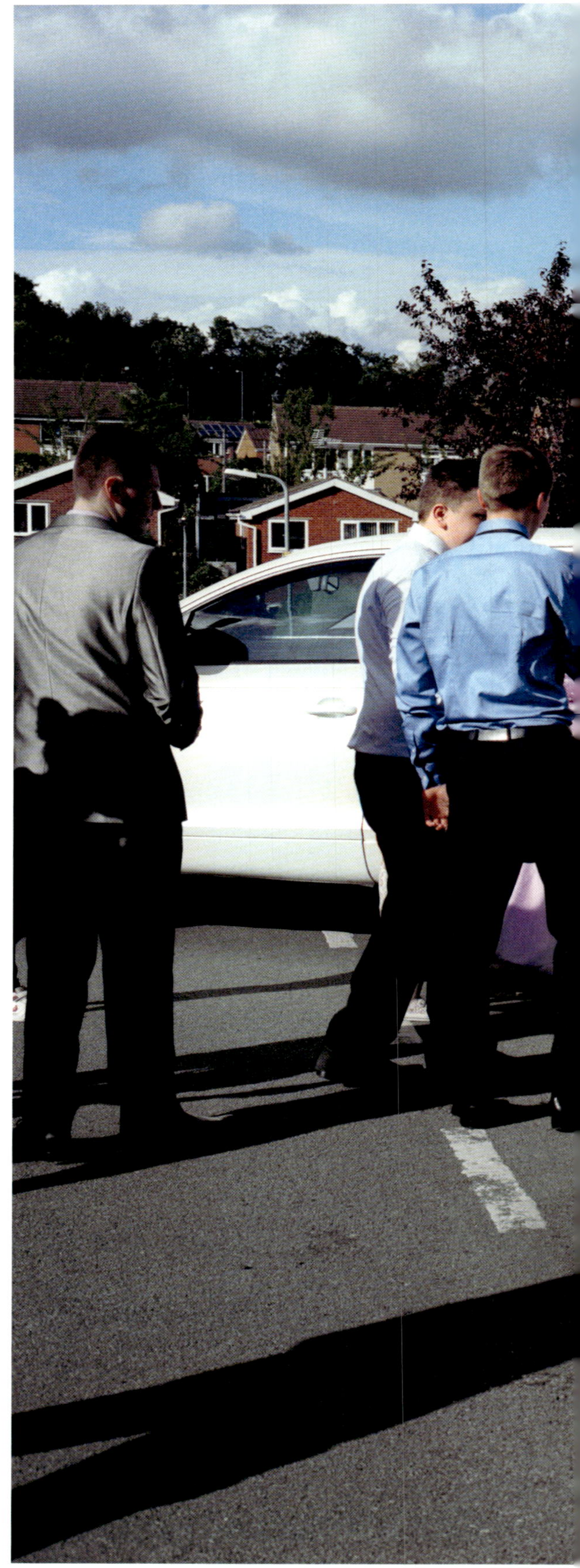

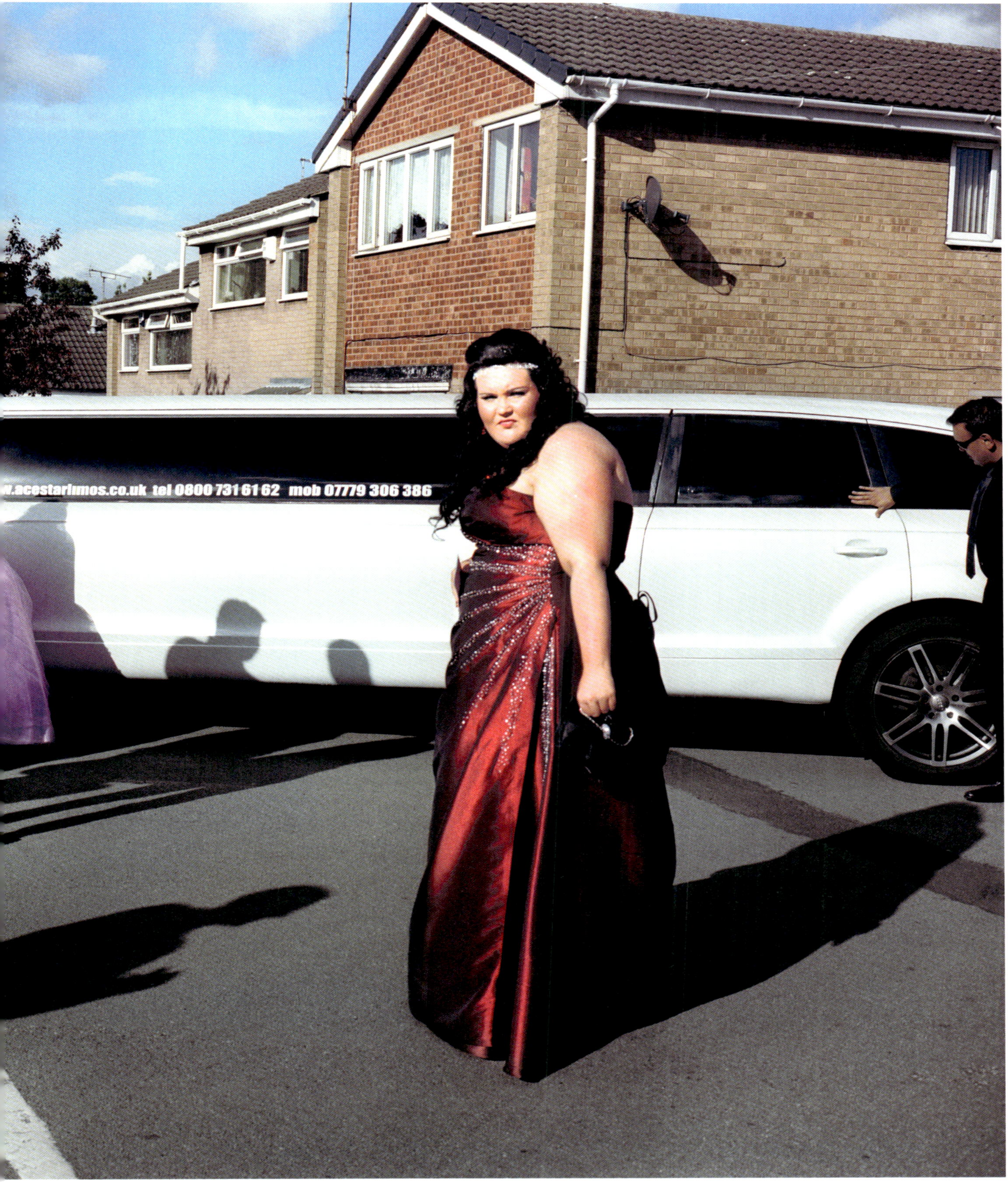
.acestarlimos.co.uk tel 0800 731 61 62 mob 07779 306 386

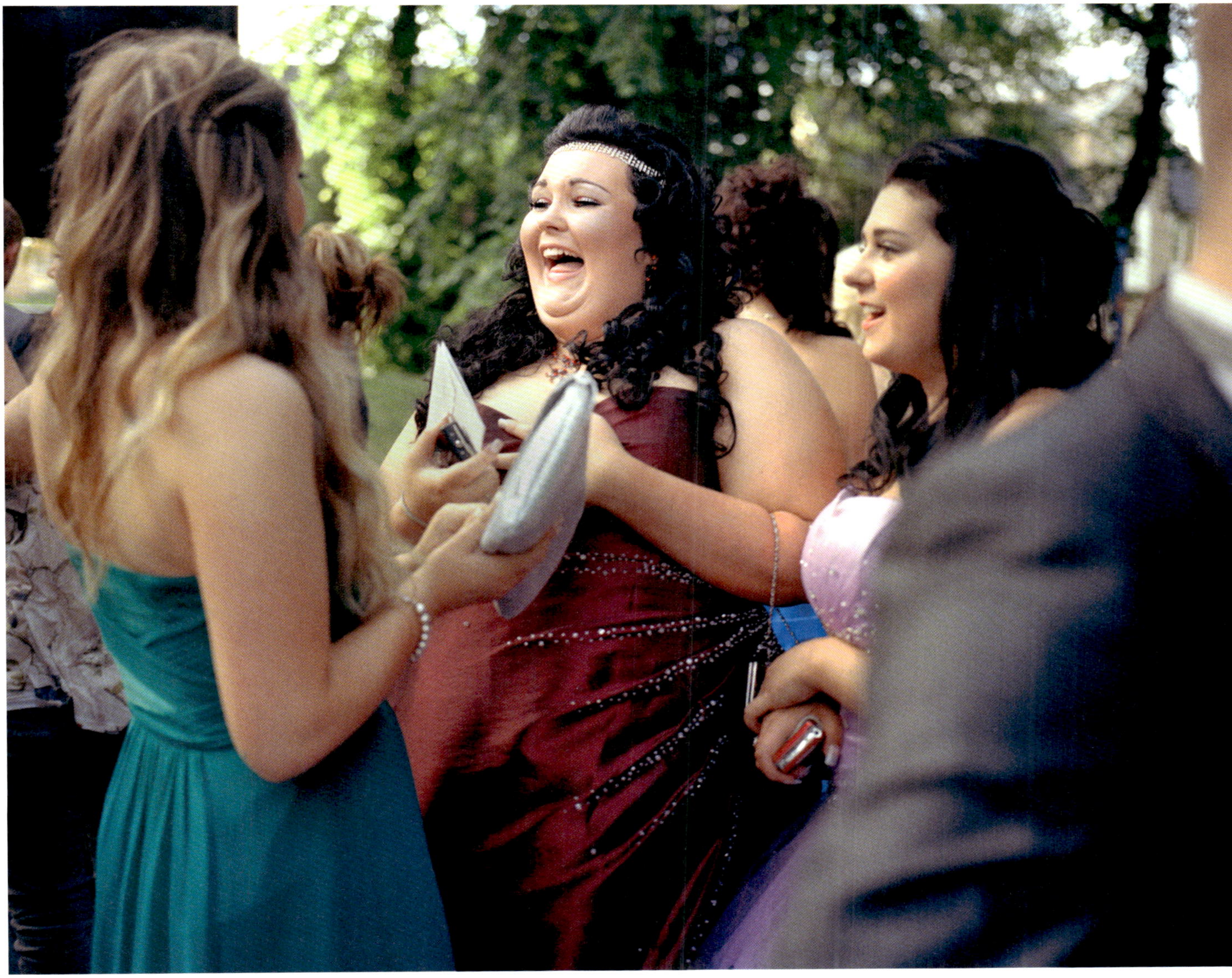

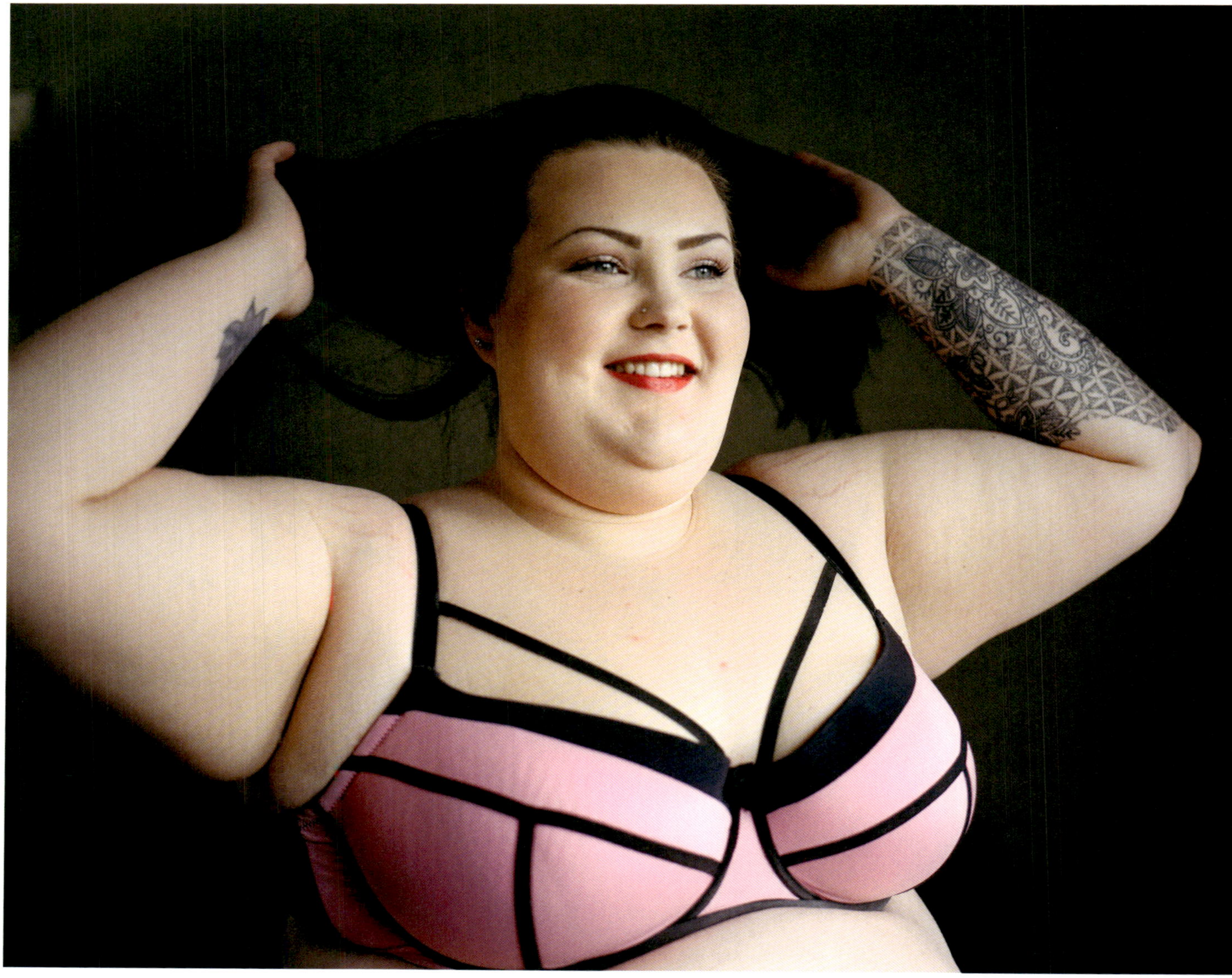

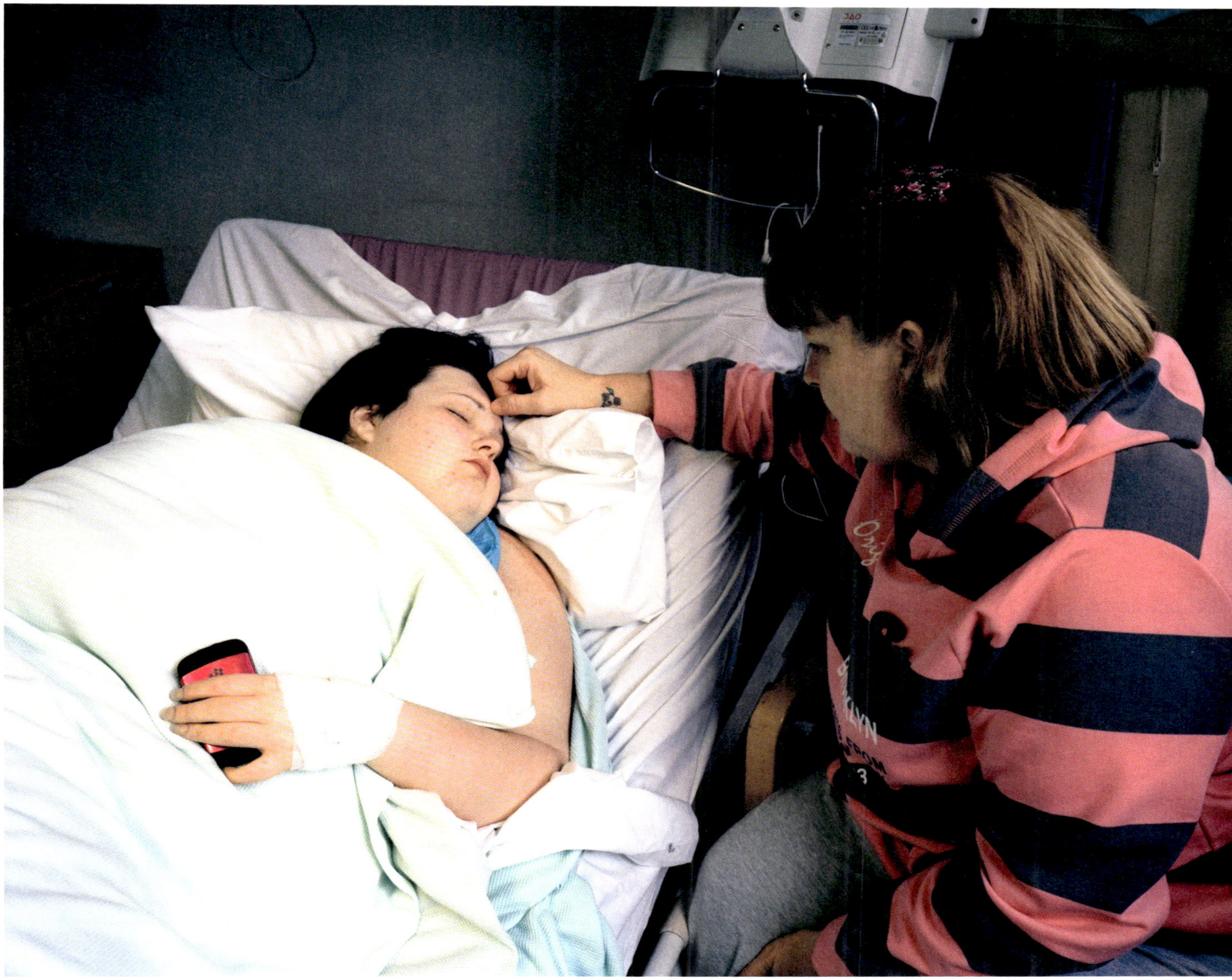

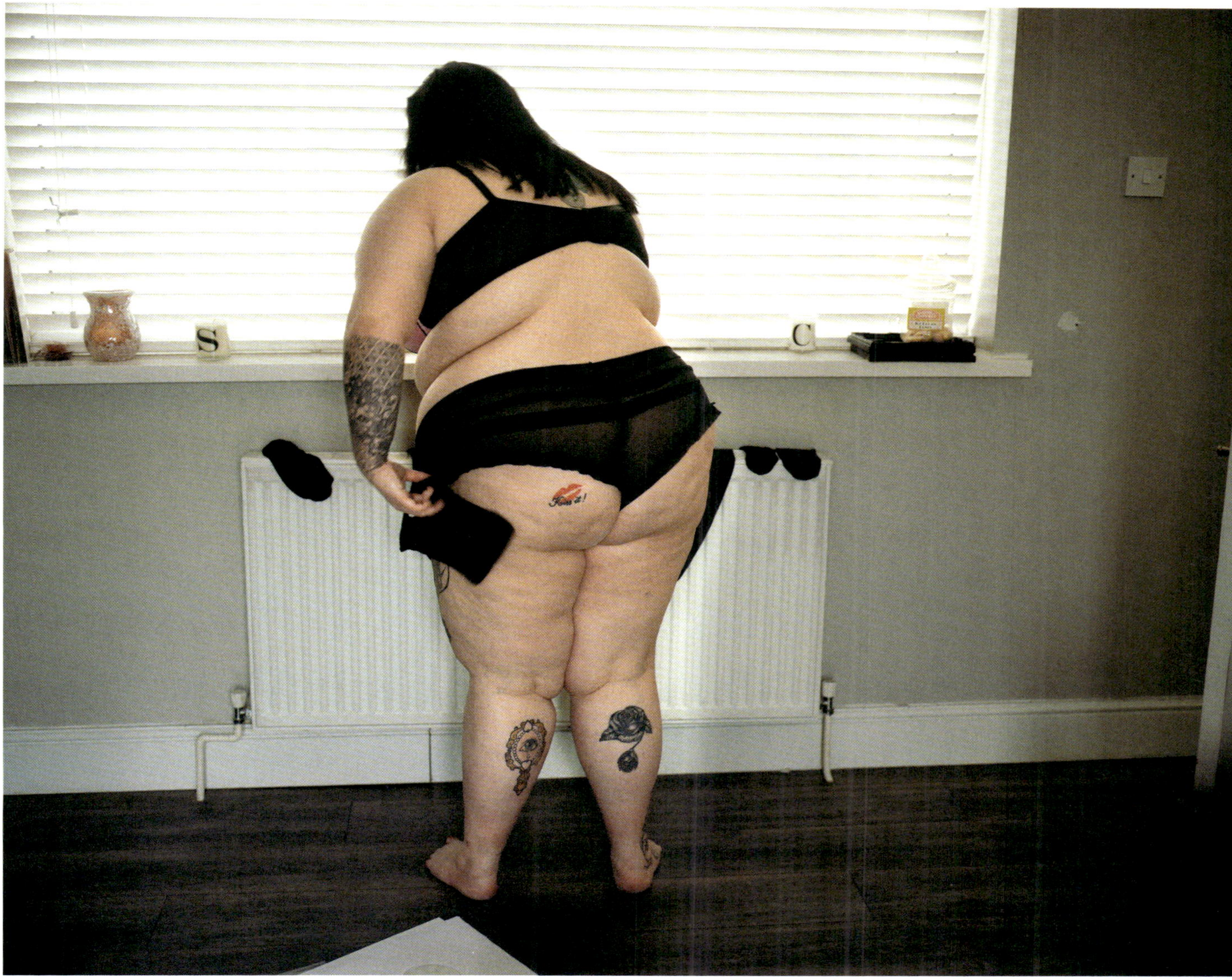
S
C

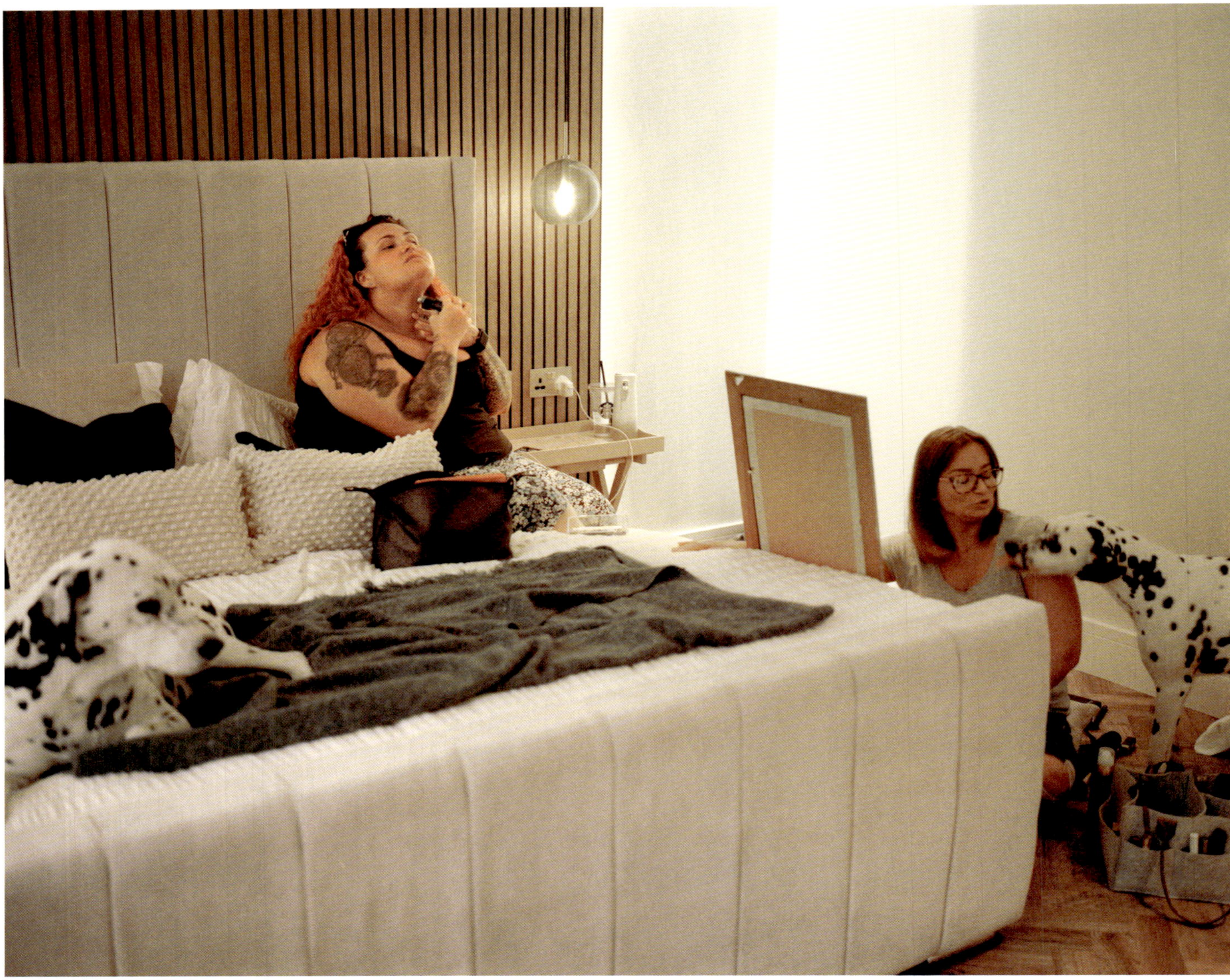

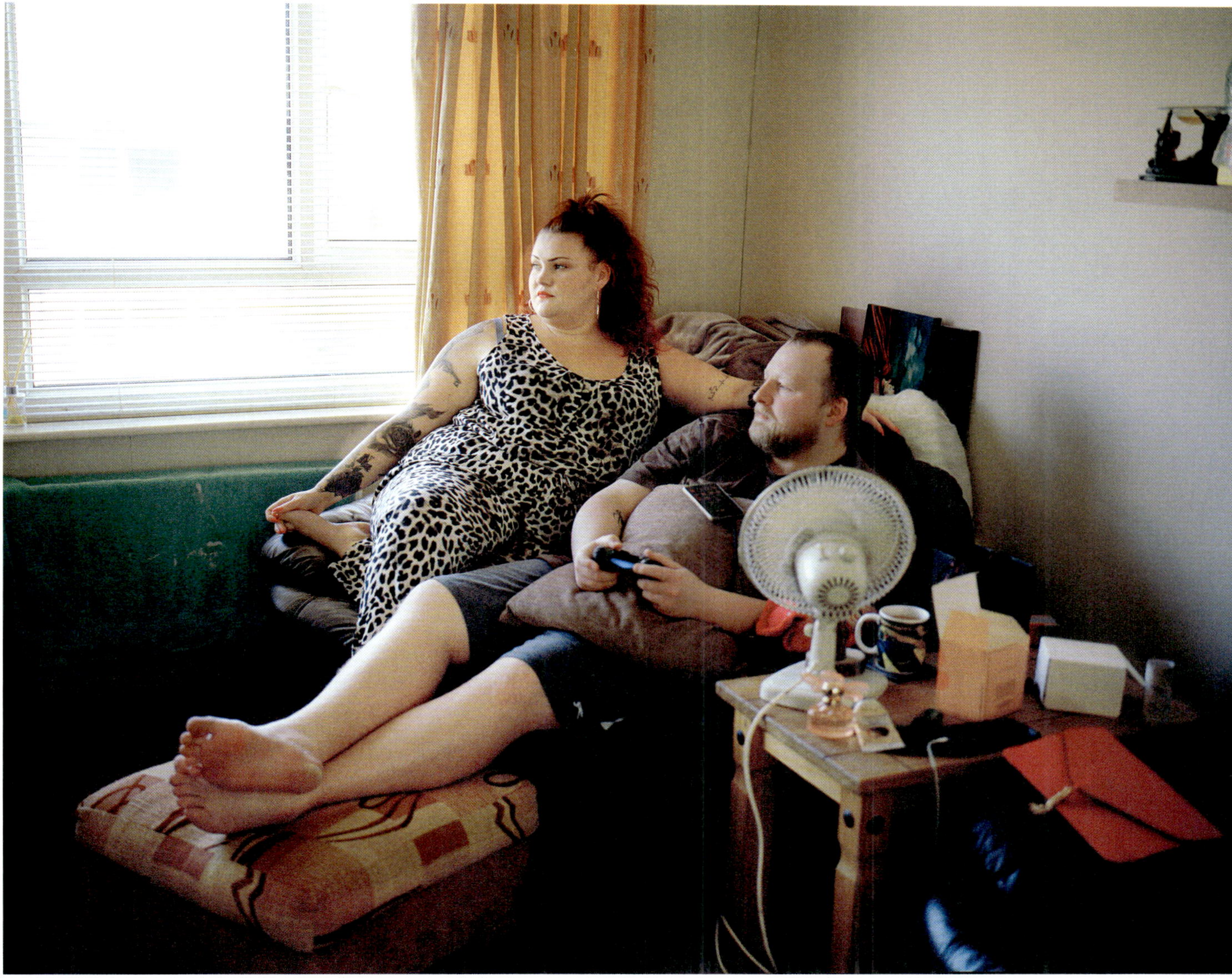

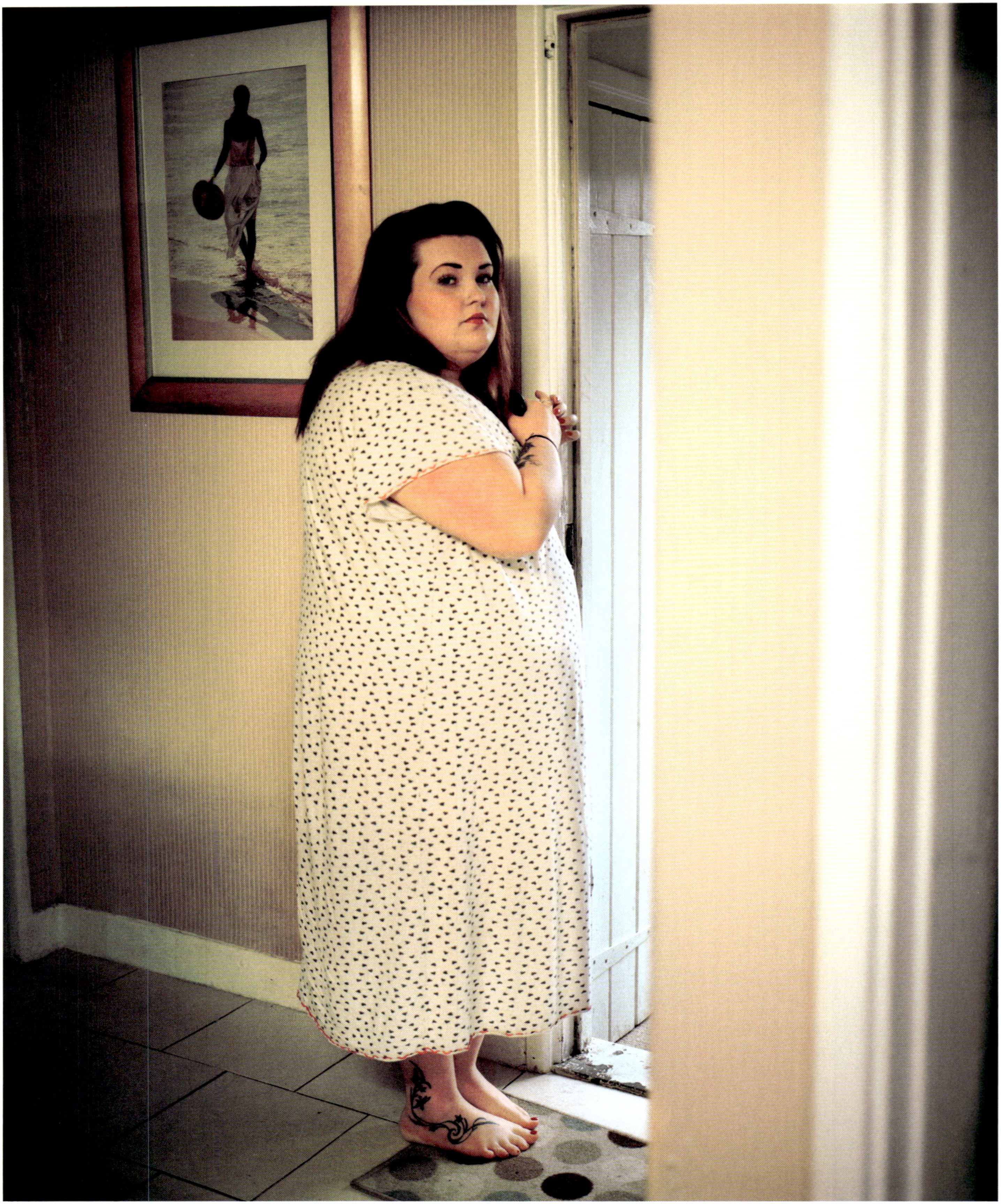

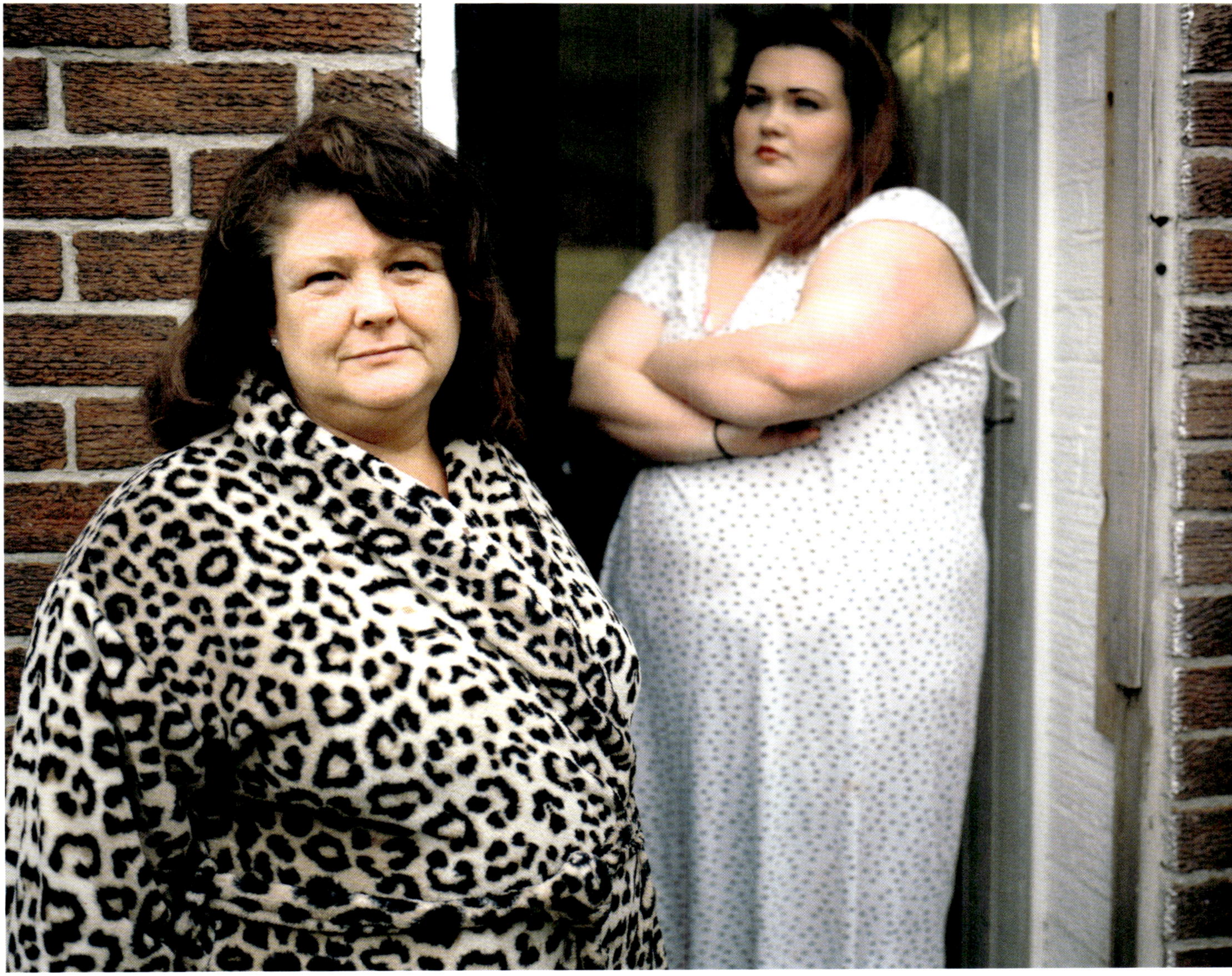

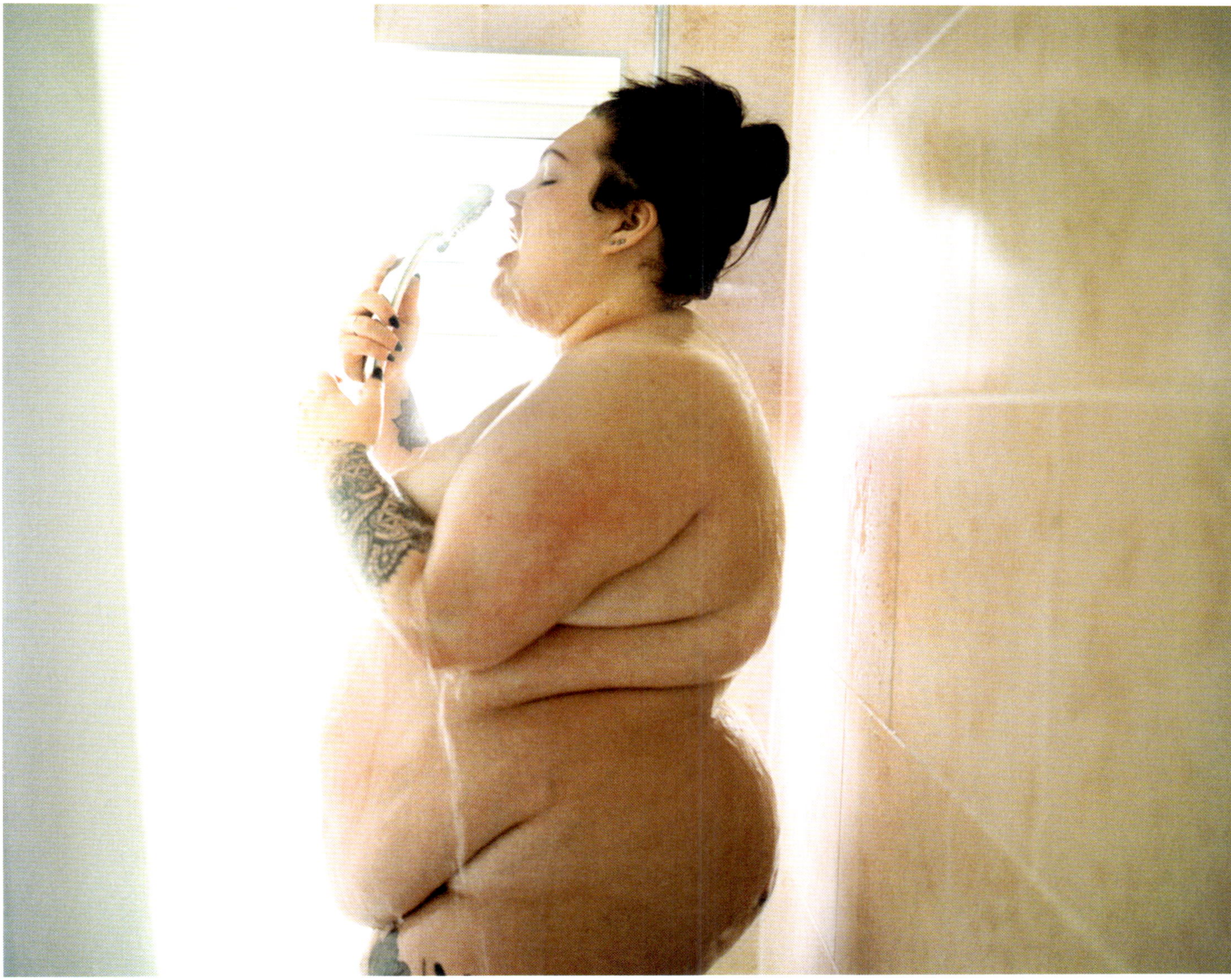

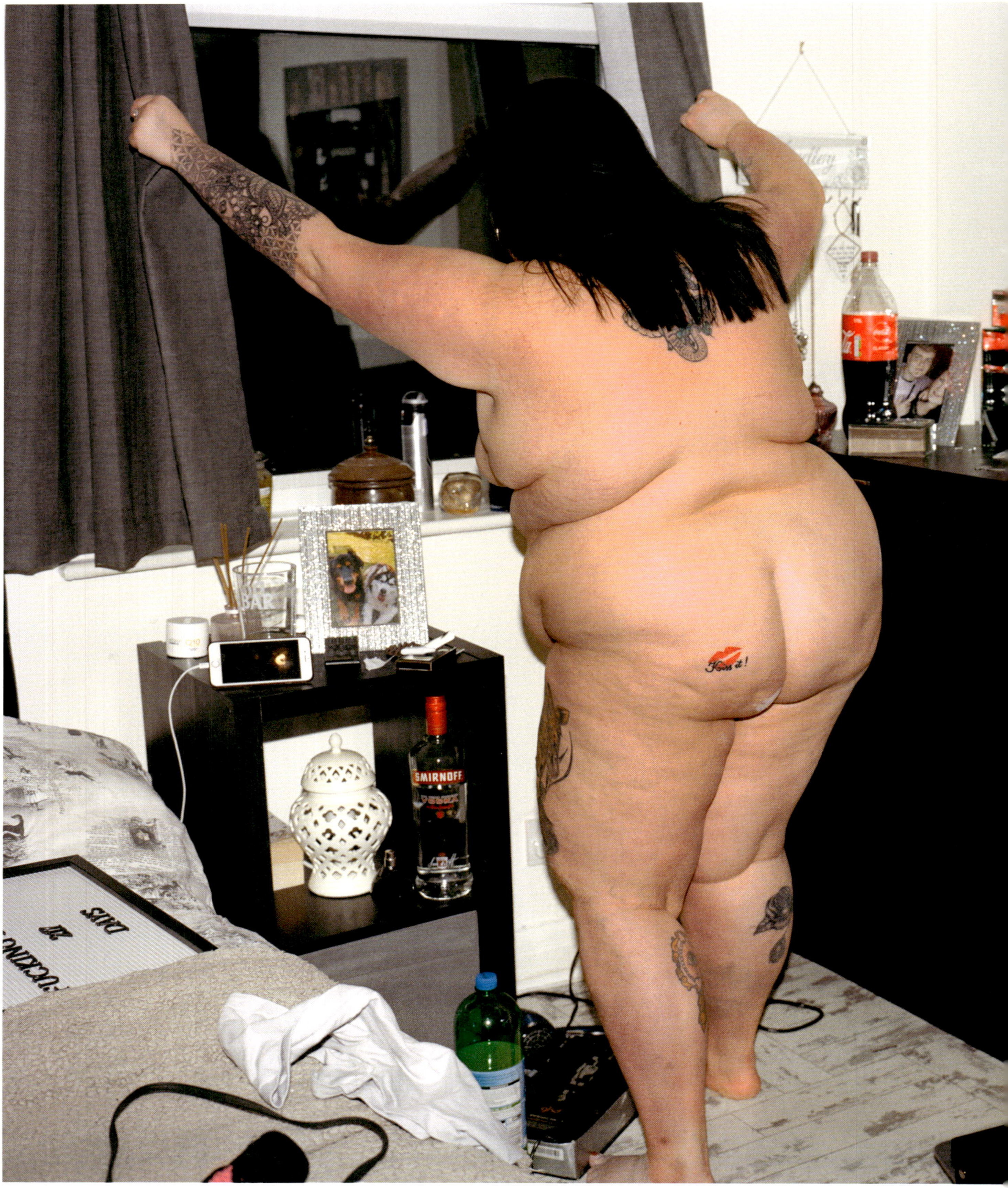
SMIRNOFF

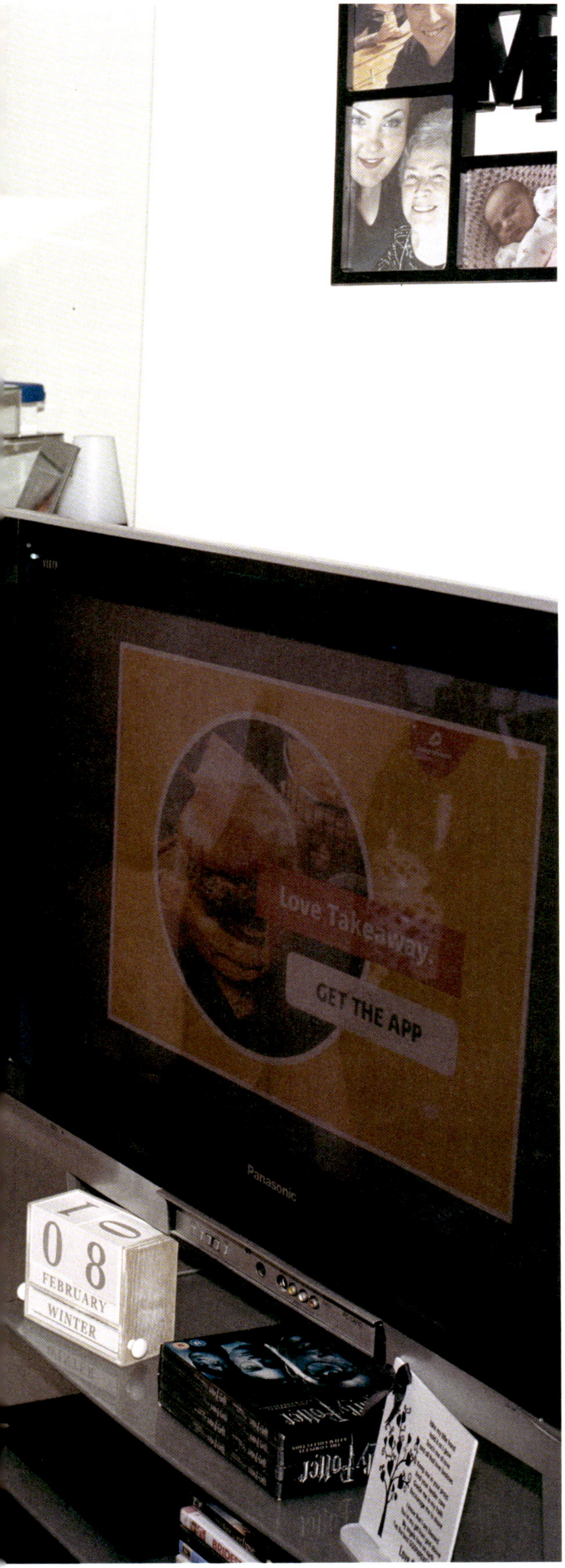
Love Takeaway.
GET THE APP
Panasonic
08
FEBRUARY
WINTER

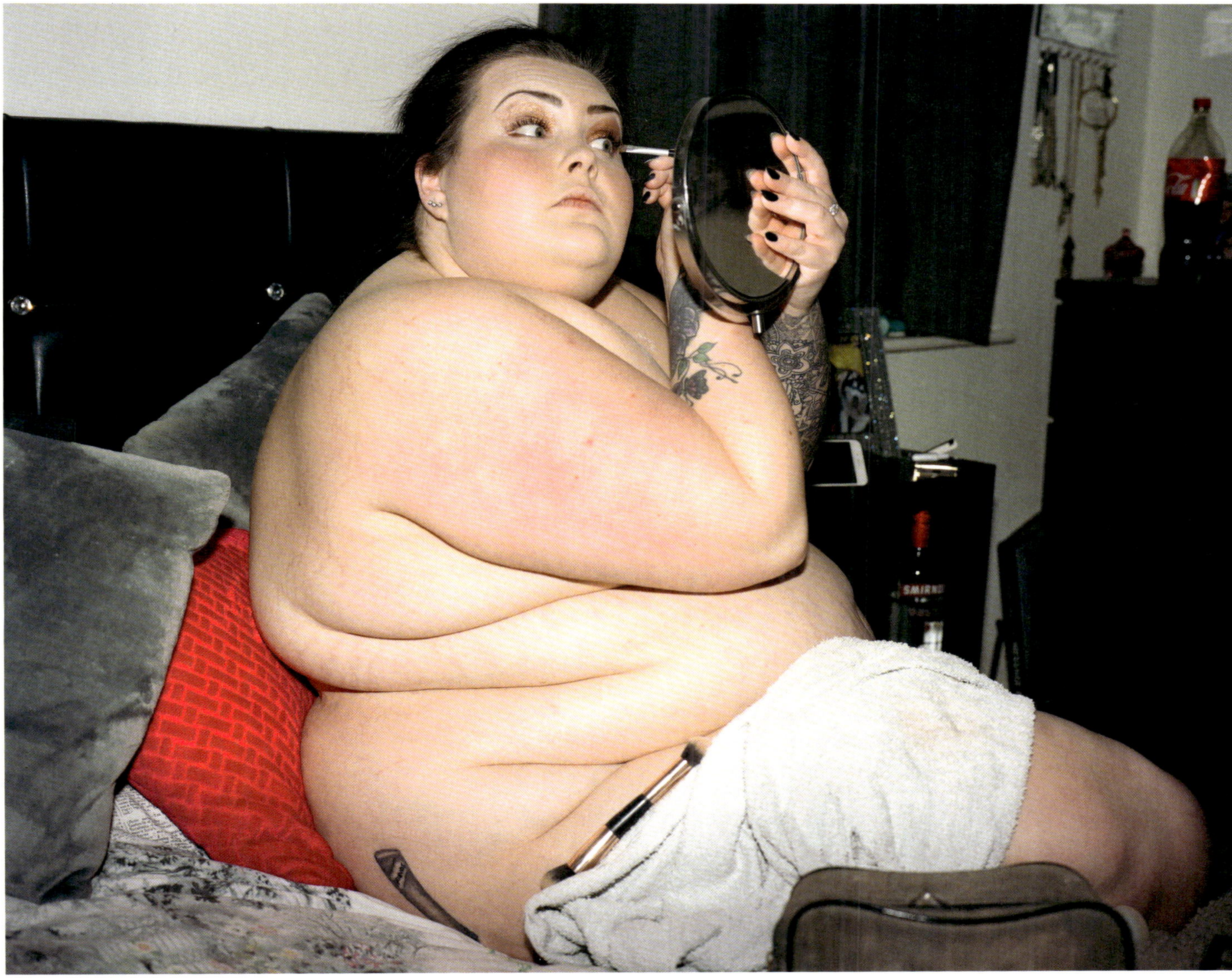

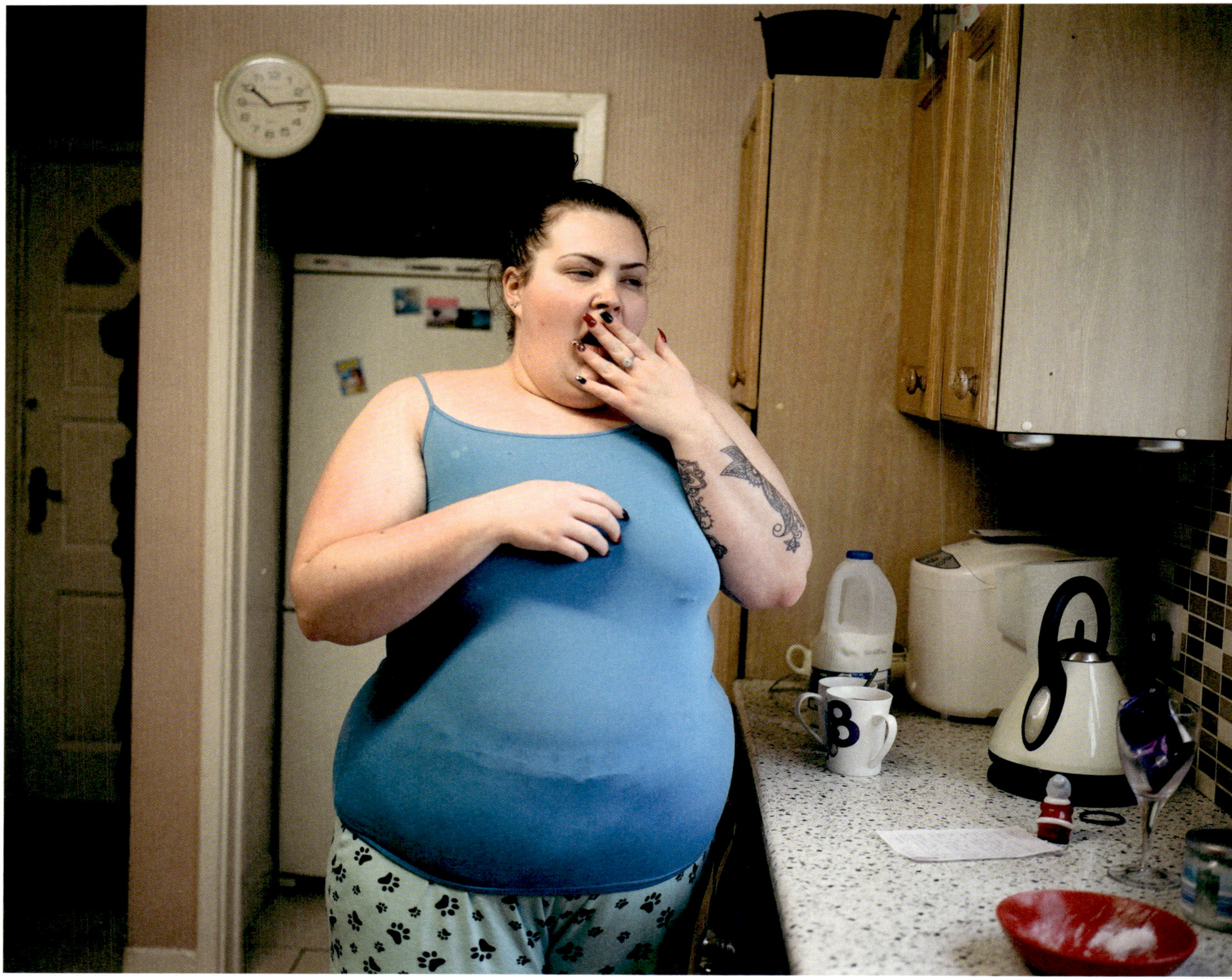

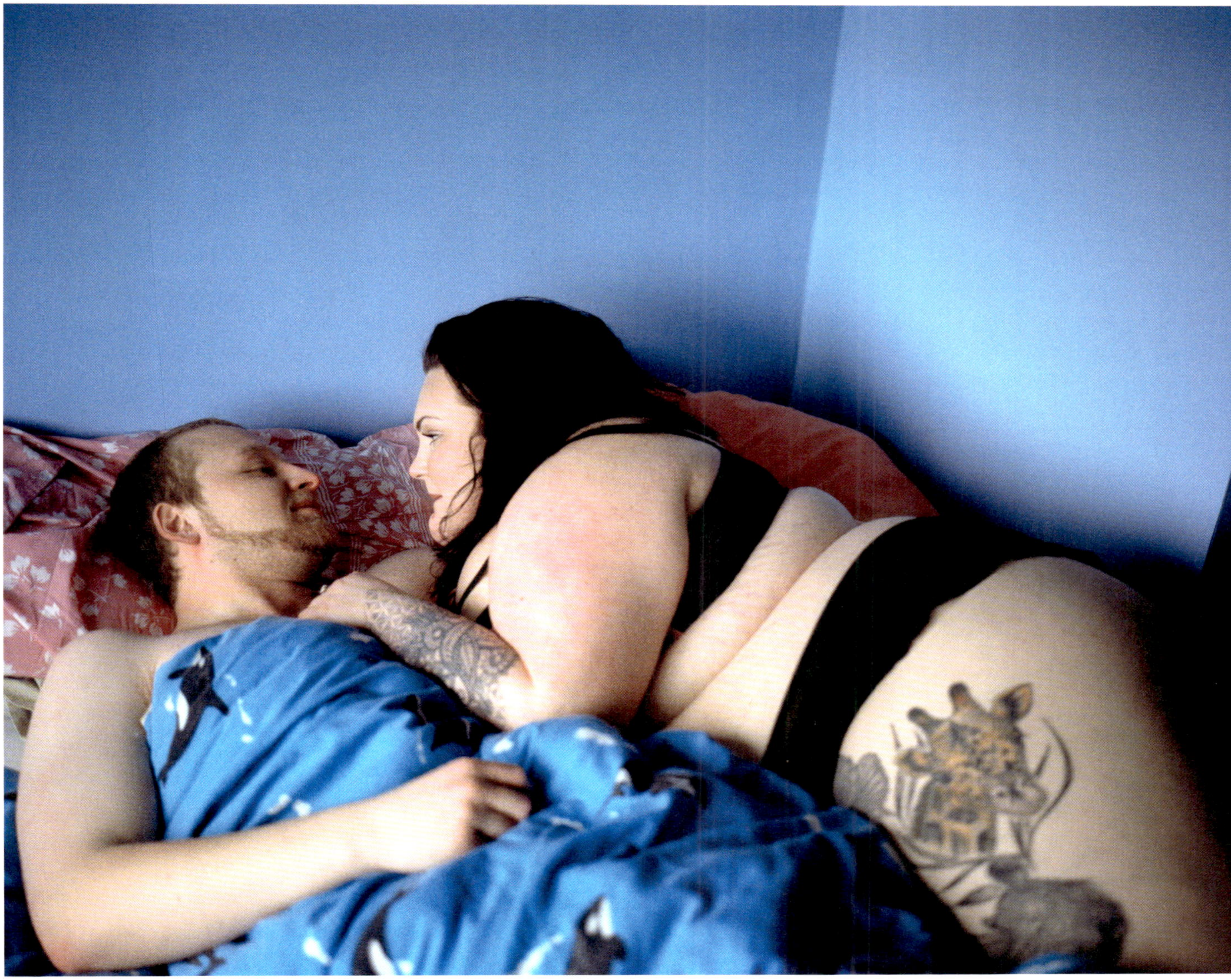

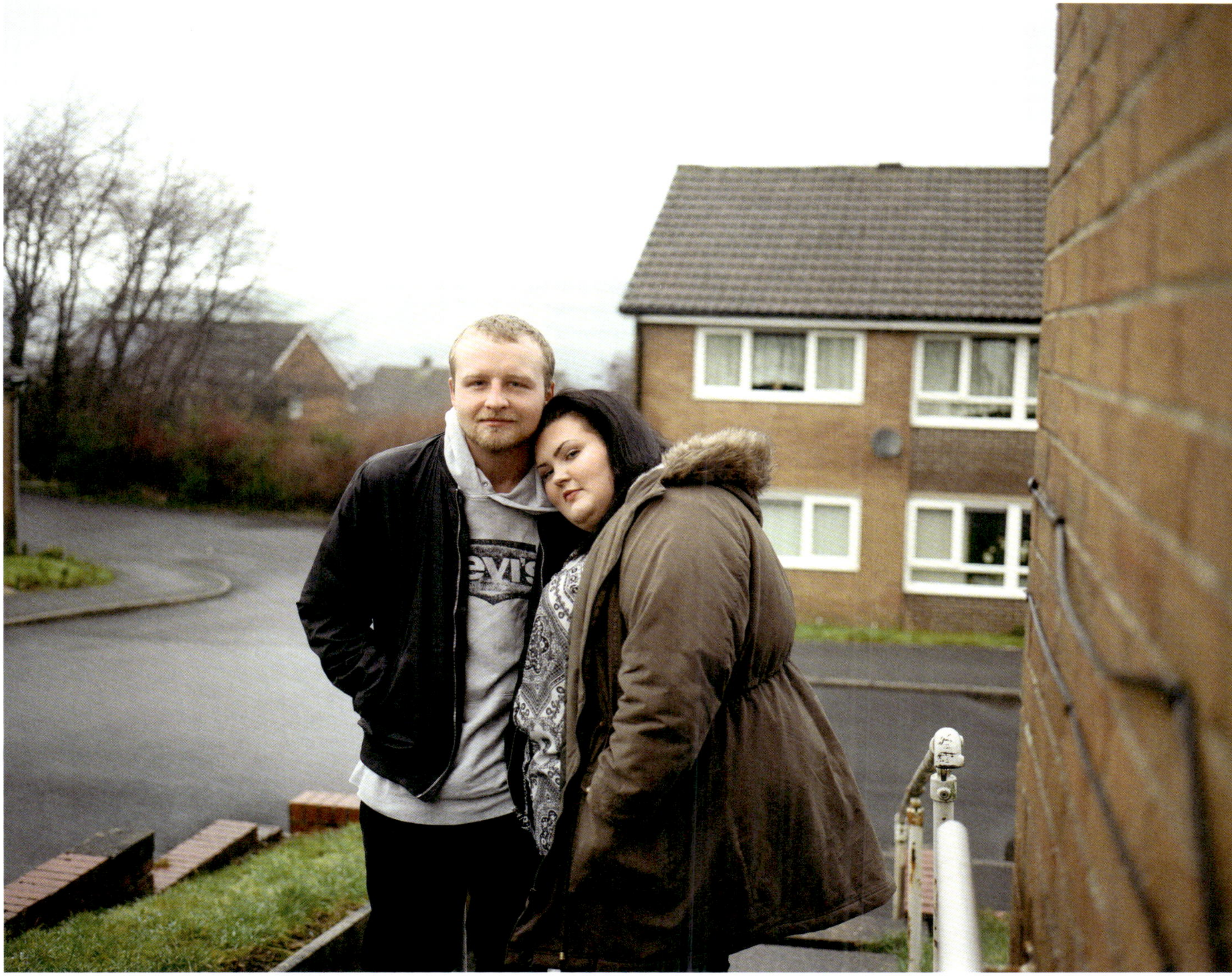

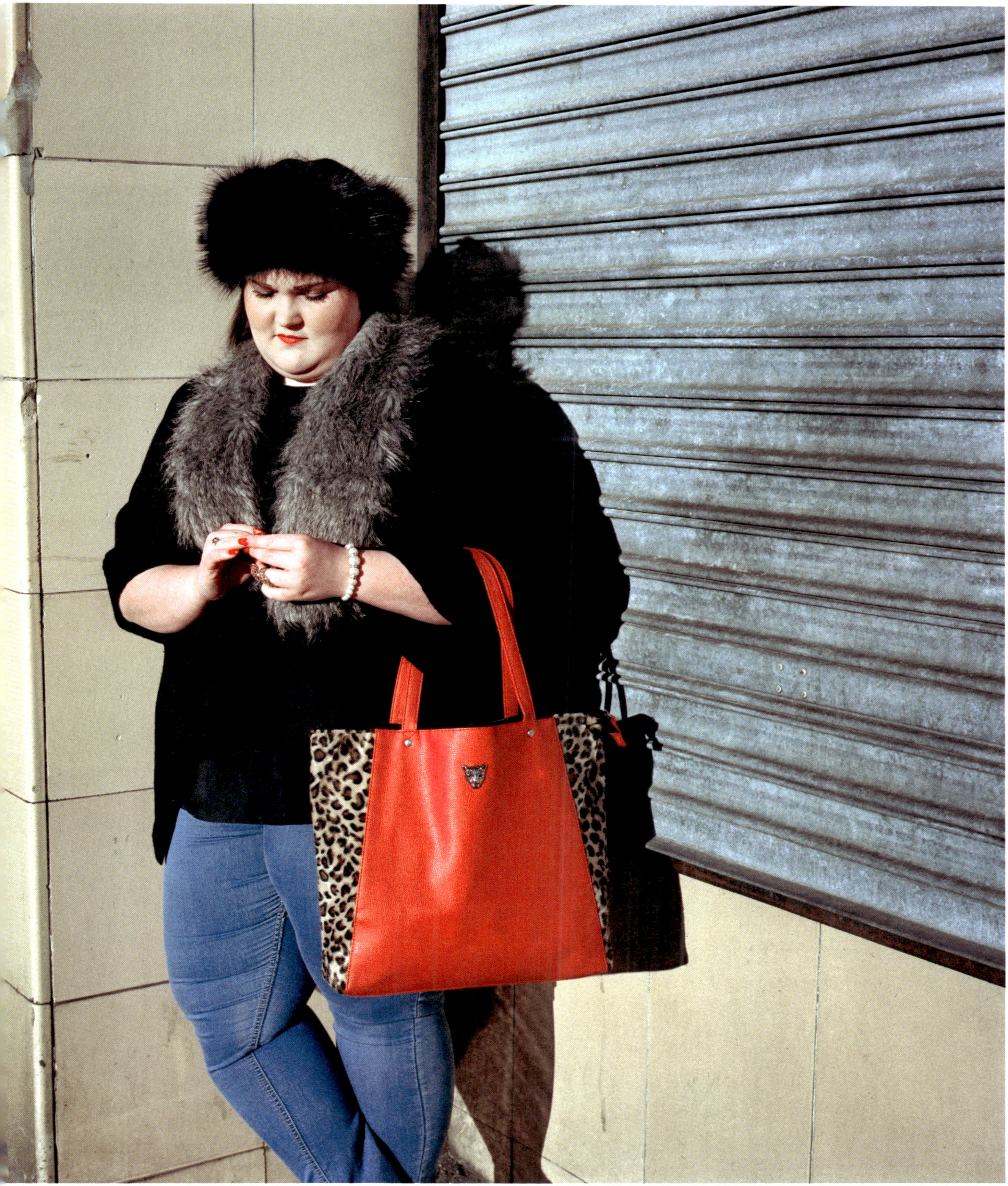

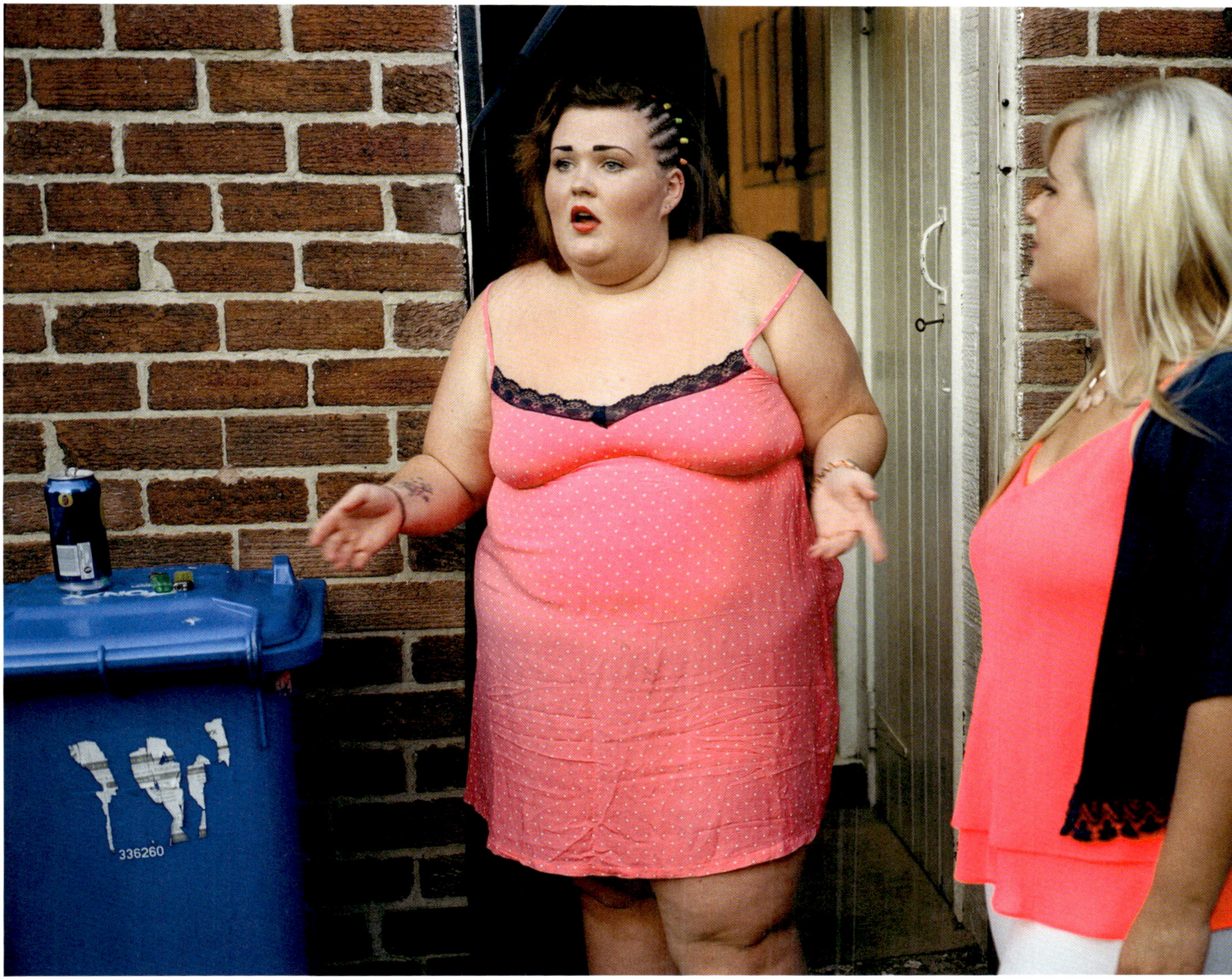
336260

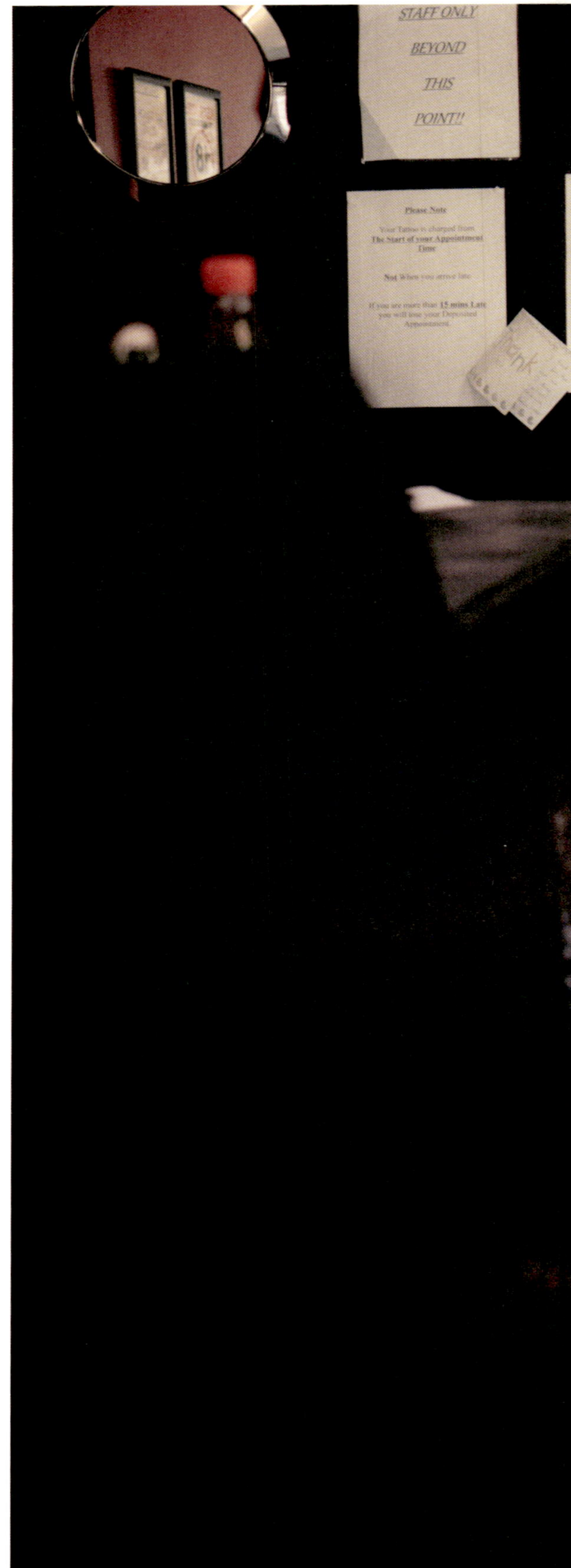
STAFF ONLY
BEYOND
THIS
POINT!!
Please Note

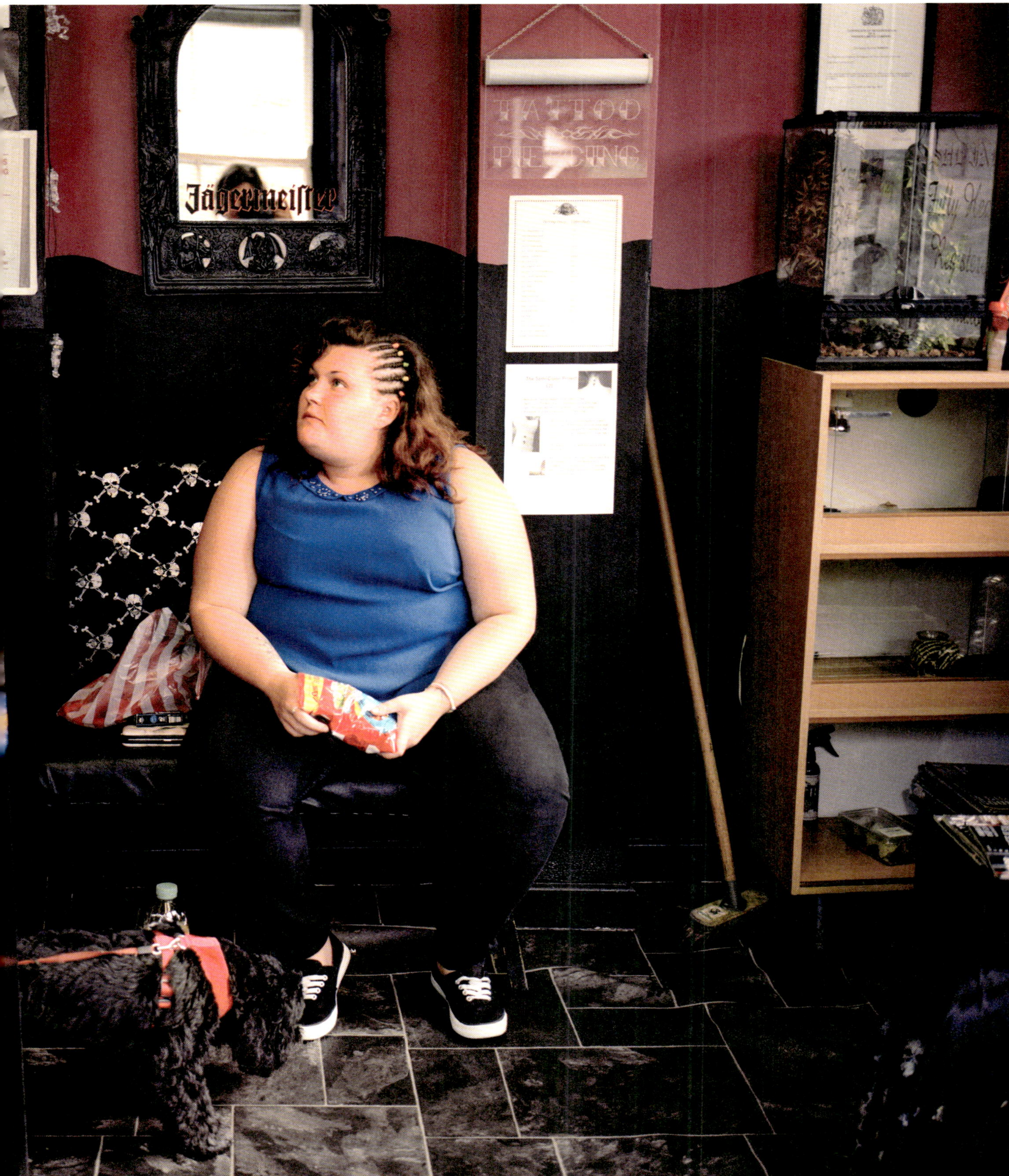
Jägermeister
TATTOO

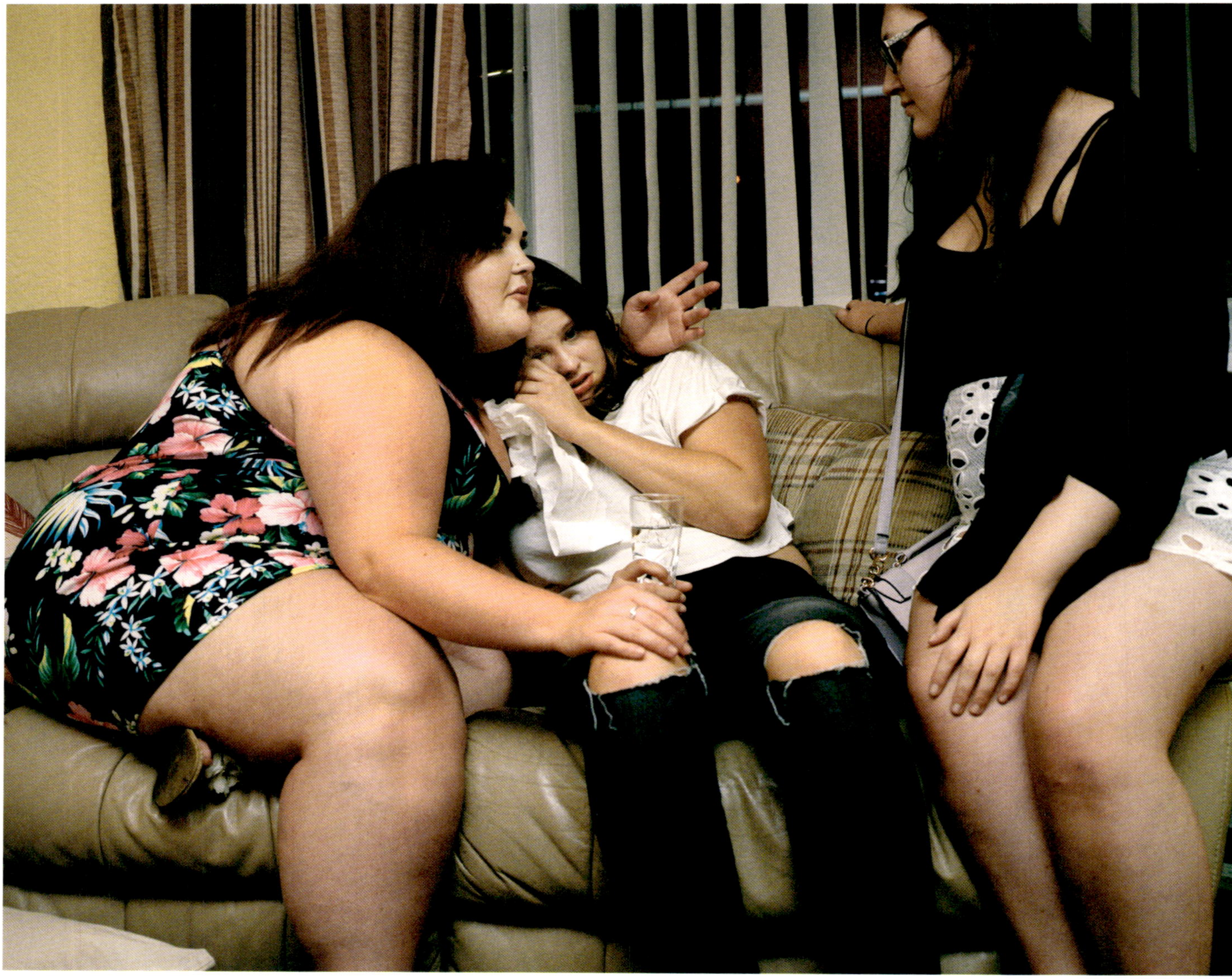

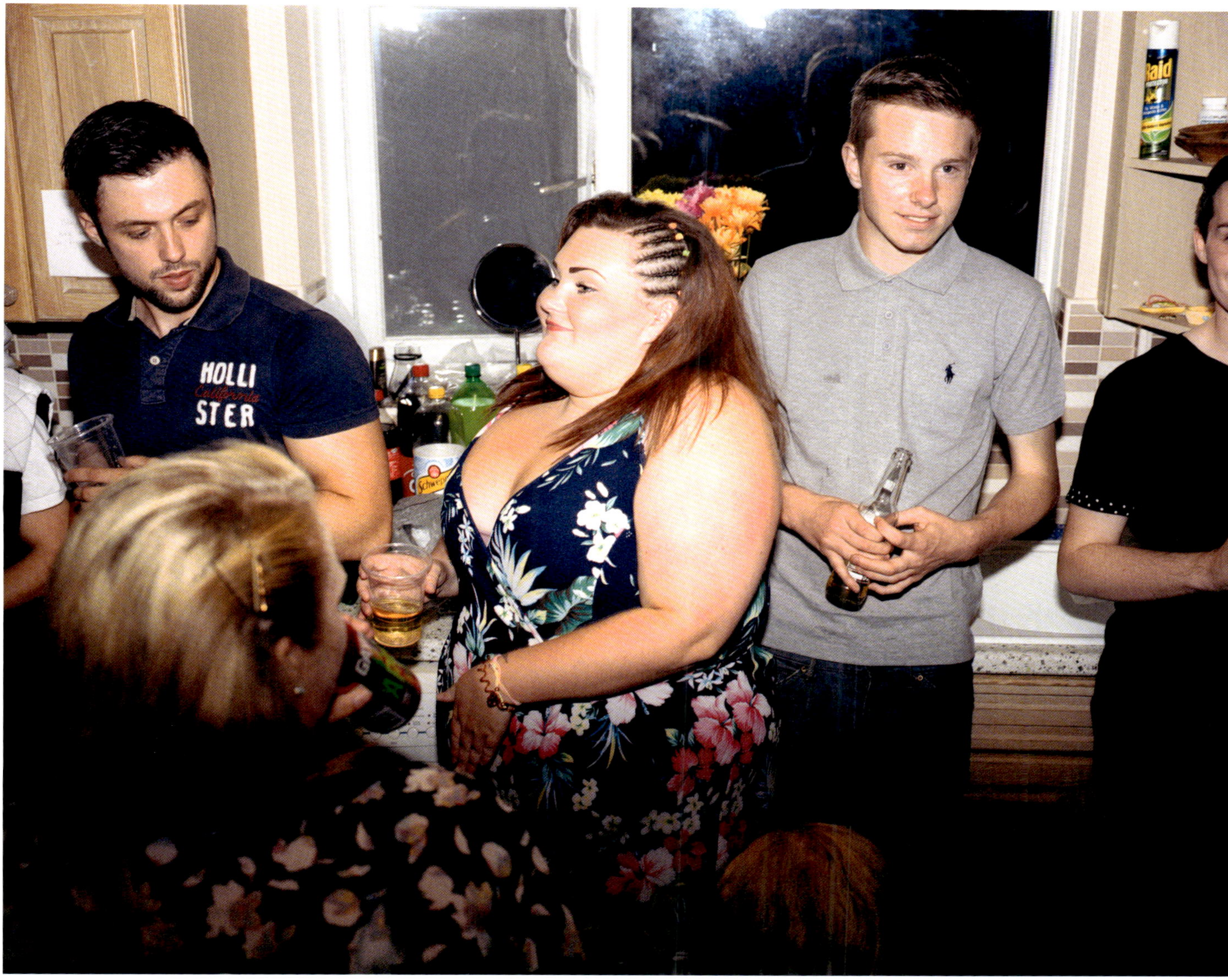
HOLLI
California
STER
Raid

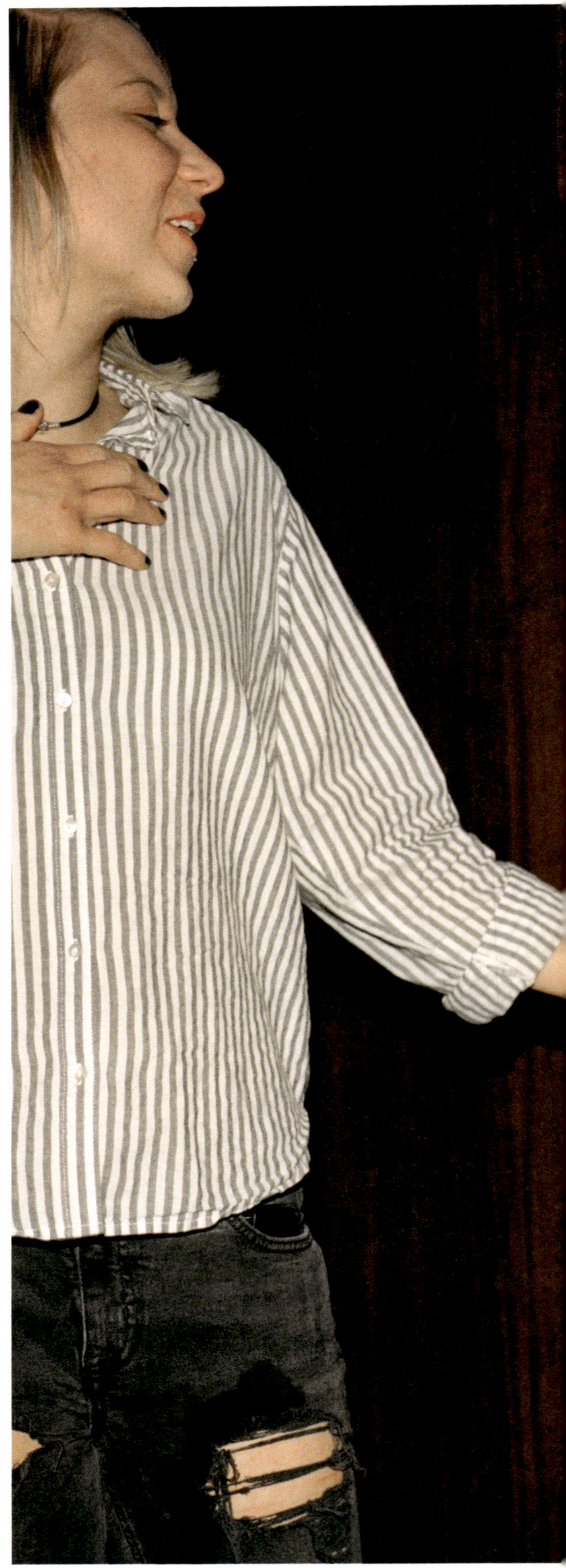

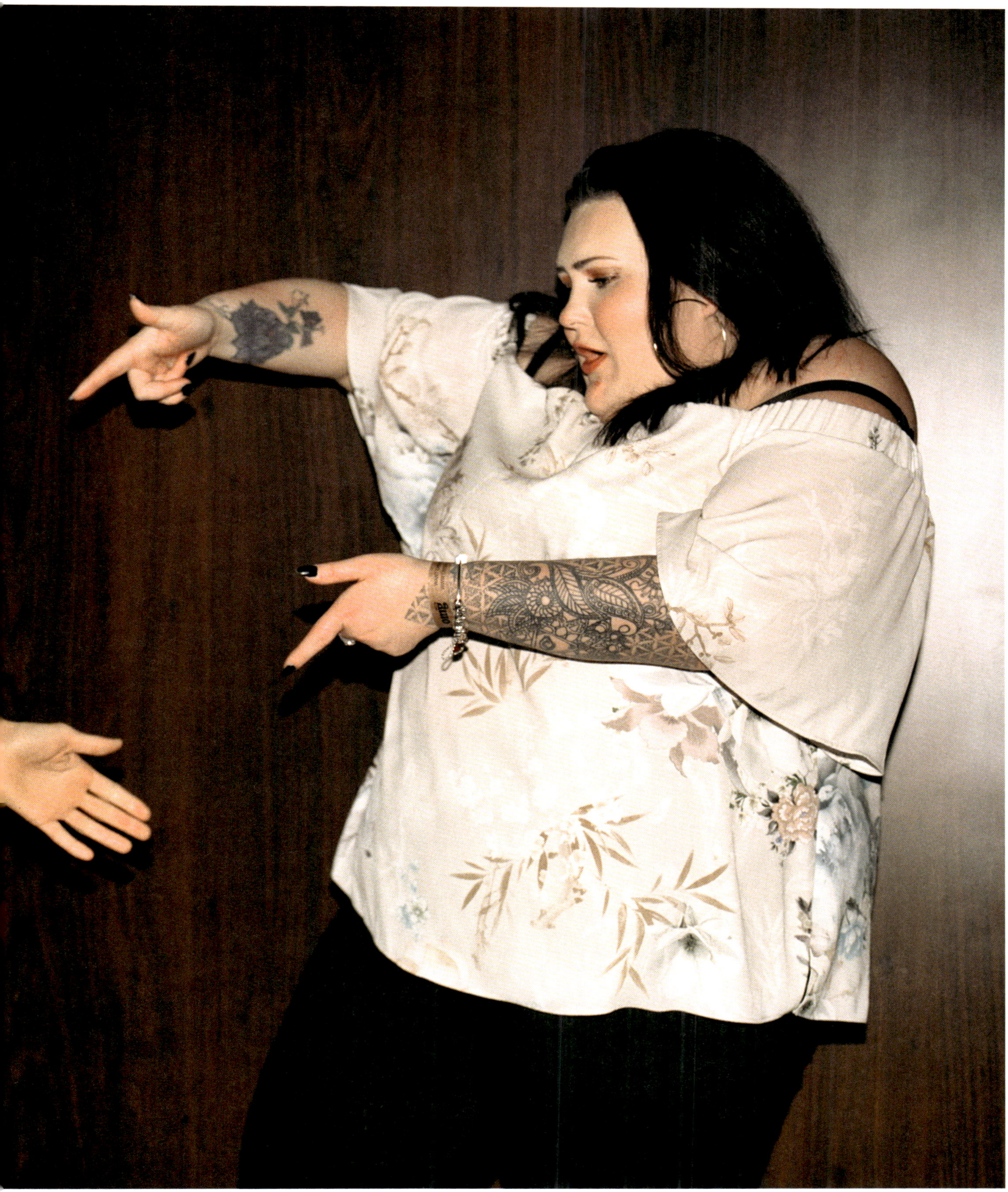

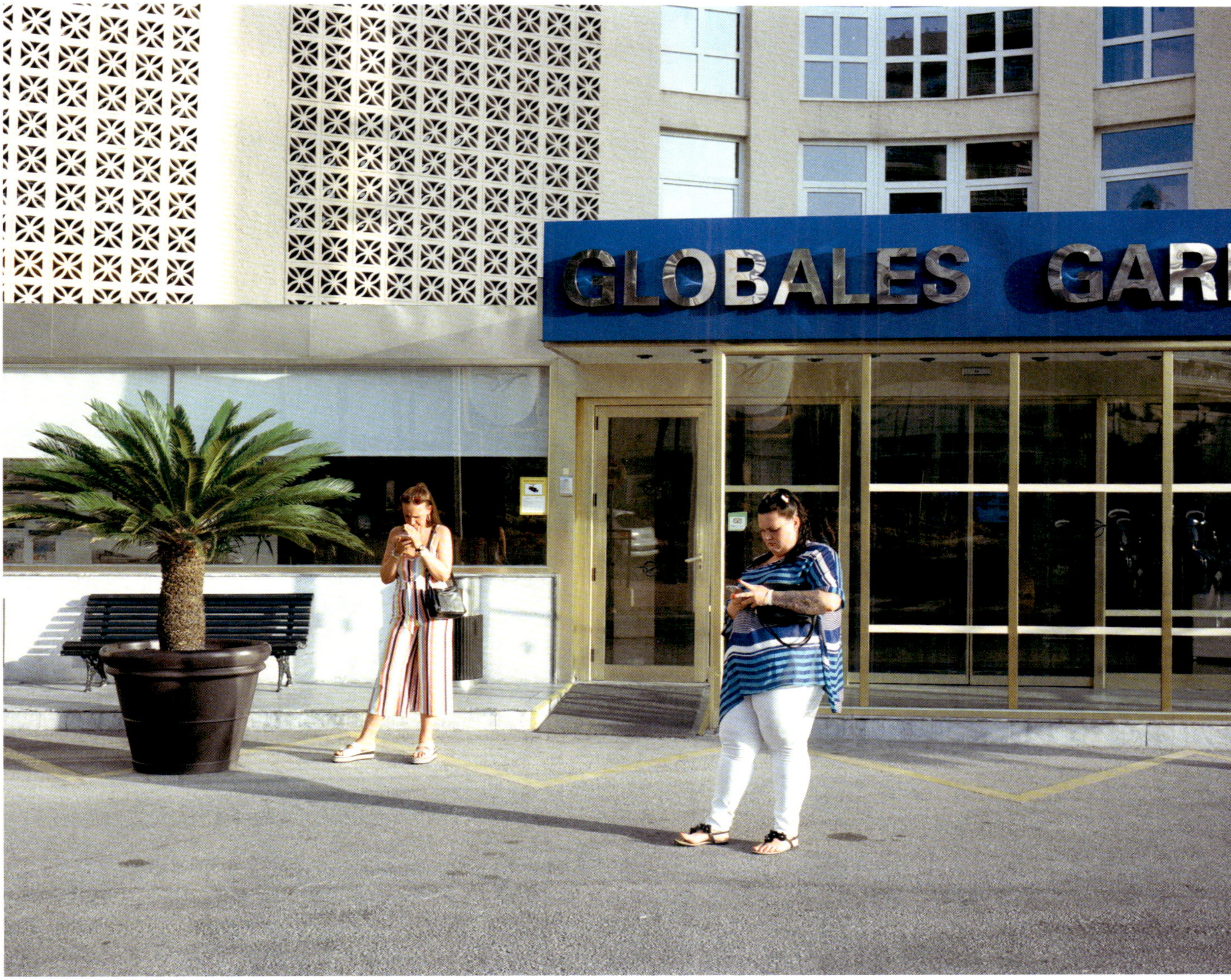
GLOBALES GAR

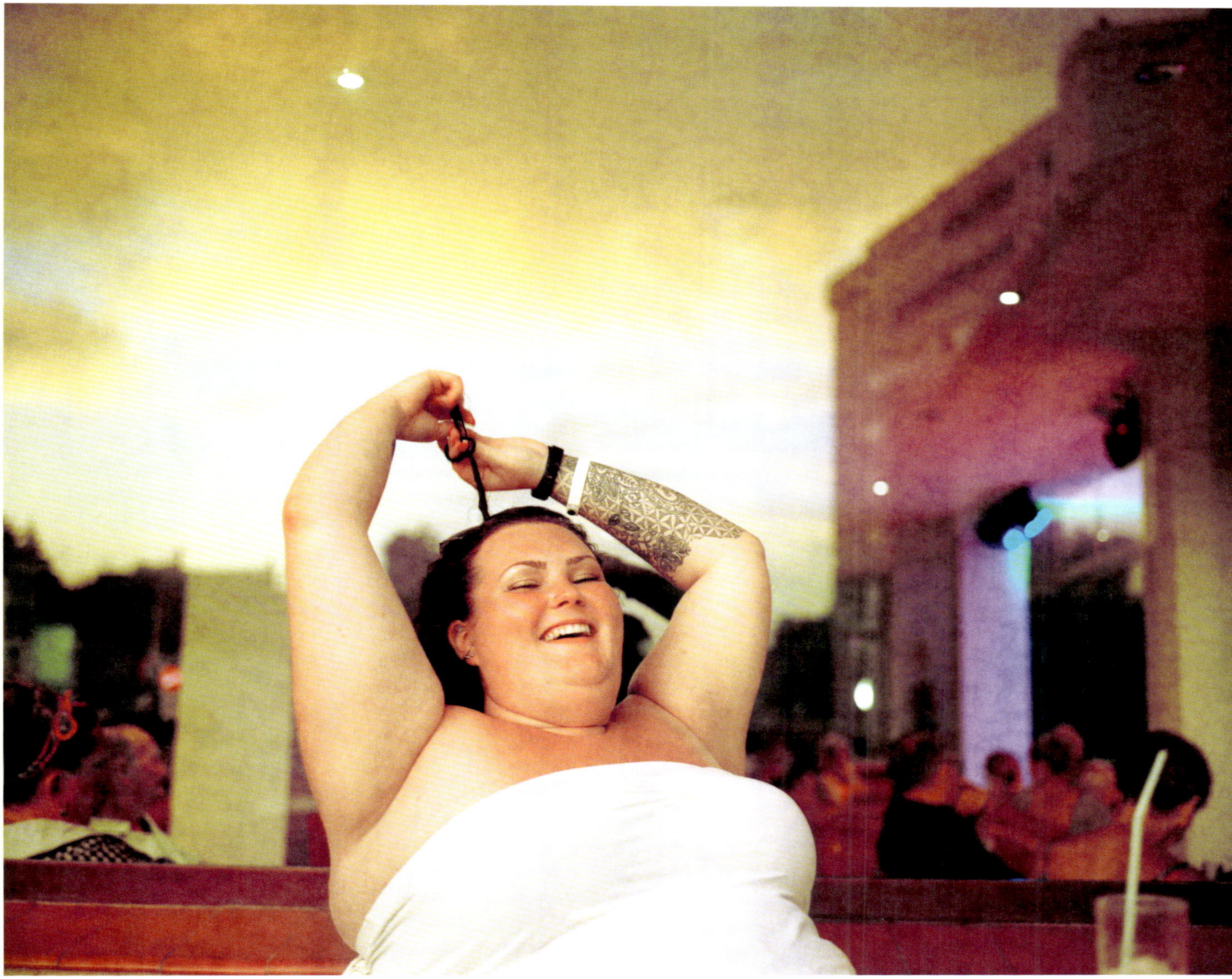

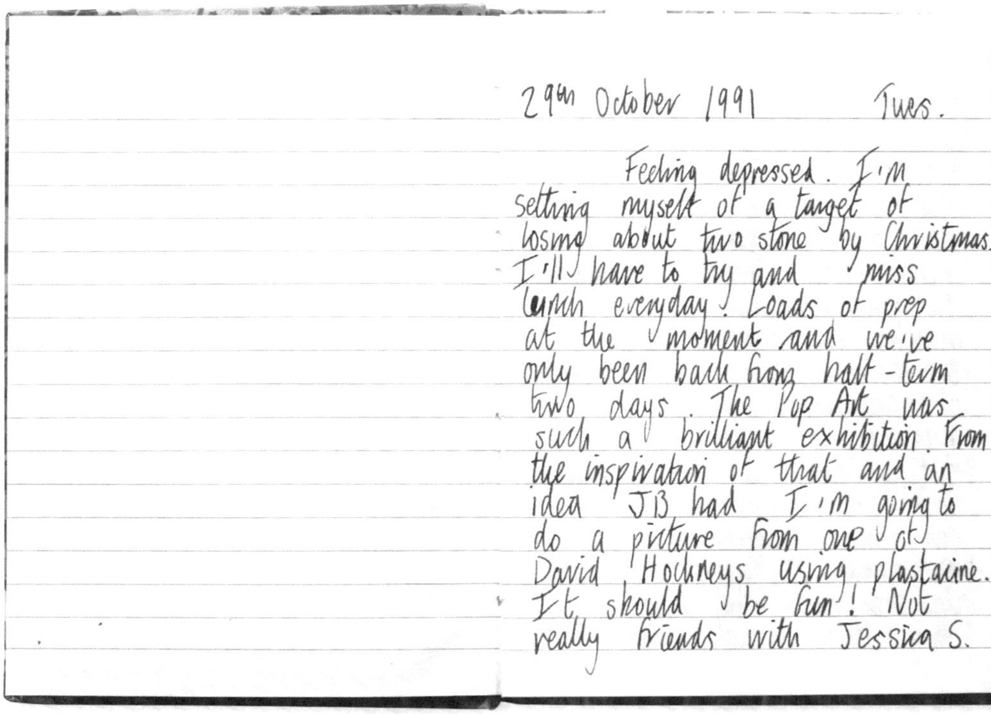

29th October 1991 Tues.

Feeling depressed. I'm setting myself of a target of losing about two stone by Christmas. I'll have to try and miss lunch everyday! Loads of prep at the moment and we've only been back from half-term two days. The Pop Art was such a brilliant exhibition. From the inspiration of that and an idea JB had I'm going to do a picture from one of David Hockneys using plastaine. It should be fun! Not really friends with Jessica S.

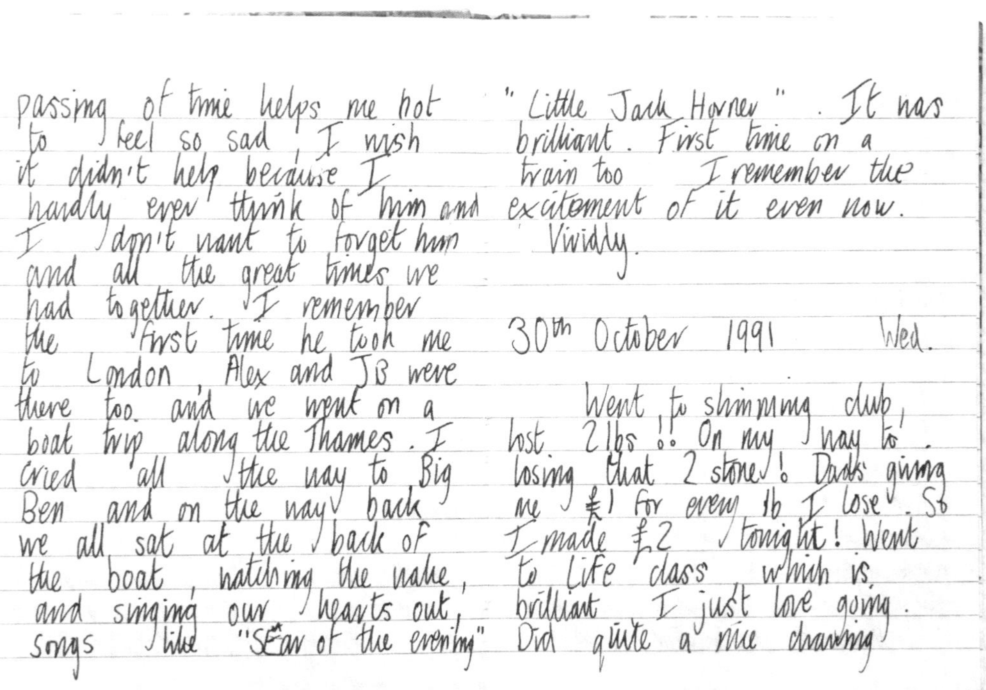

passing of time helps me not to feel so sad, I wish it didn't help because I hardly ever think of him and I don't want to forget him and all the great times we had together. I remember the first time he took me to London, Alex and JB were there too and we went on a boat trip along the Thames. I cried all the way to Big Ben and on the way back we all sat at the back of the boat, watching the wake, and singing our hearts out, songs like "Star of the evening" "Little Jack Horner". It was brilliant. First time on a train too. I remember the excitement of it even now. Vividly.

30th October 1991 Wed.

Went to slimming club, lost 2lbs!! On my way to losing that 2 stone! Dad's giving me £1 for every lb I lose. So I made £2 tonight! Went to life class which is brilliant I just love going. Did quite a nice drawing

Abbie's diaries. Age 14, 1991

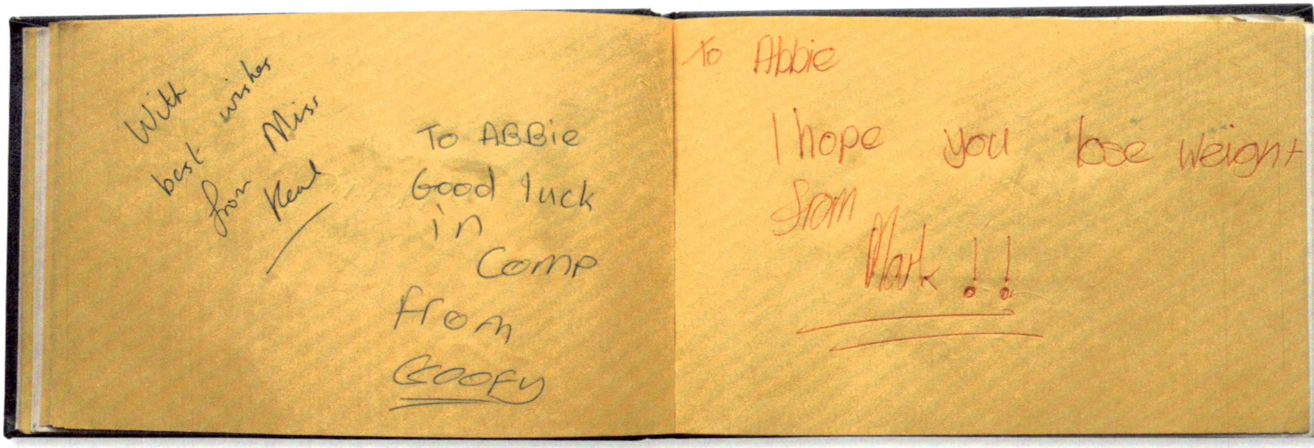

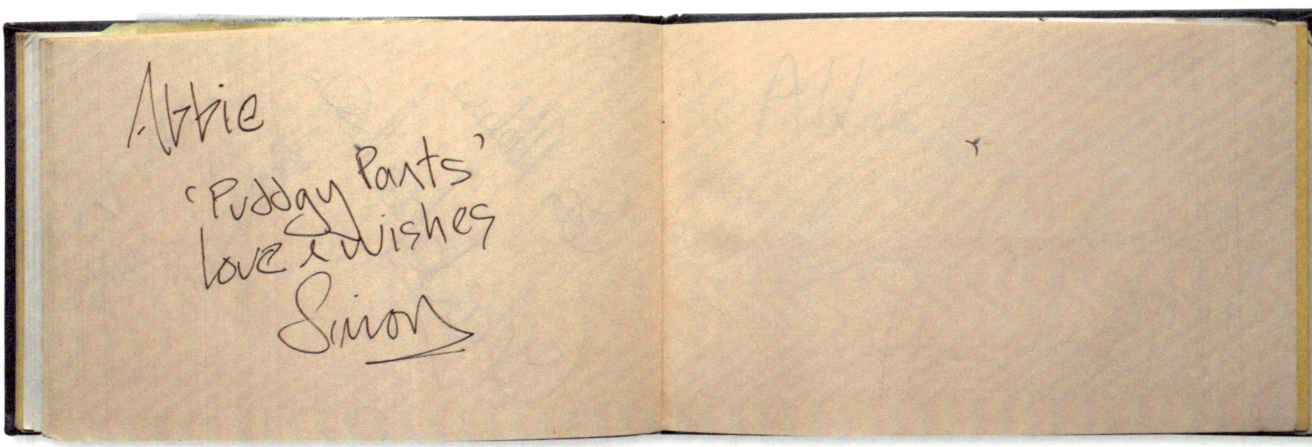

Abbie's autograph book. Age 11, 1988
Top: Messages were collected from class mates as she left junior school to go on to secondary school.
Bottom: She also asked family members to sign her book.

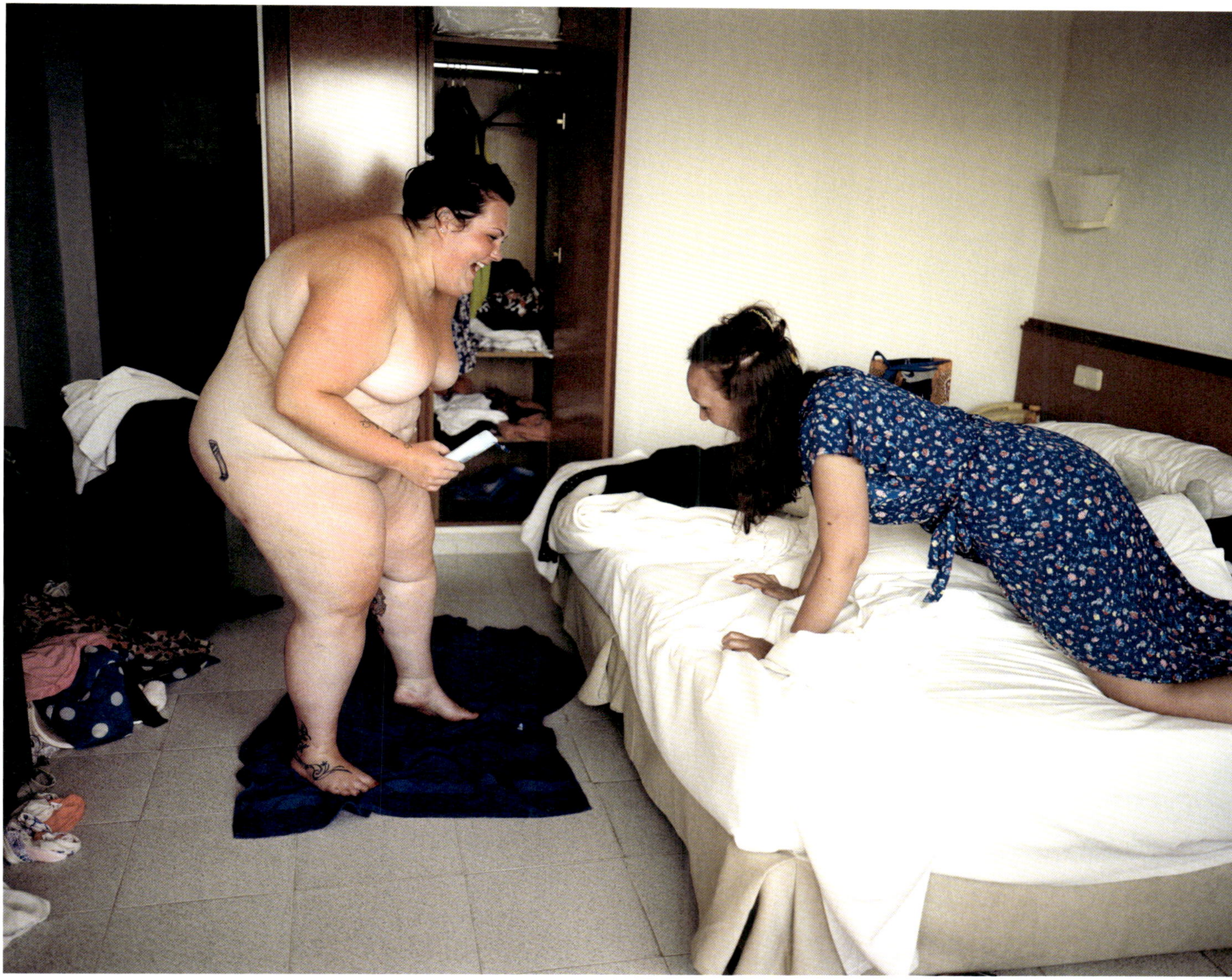

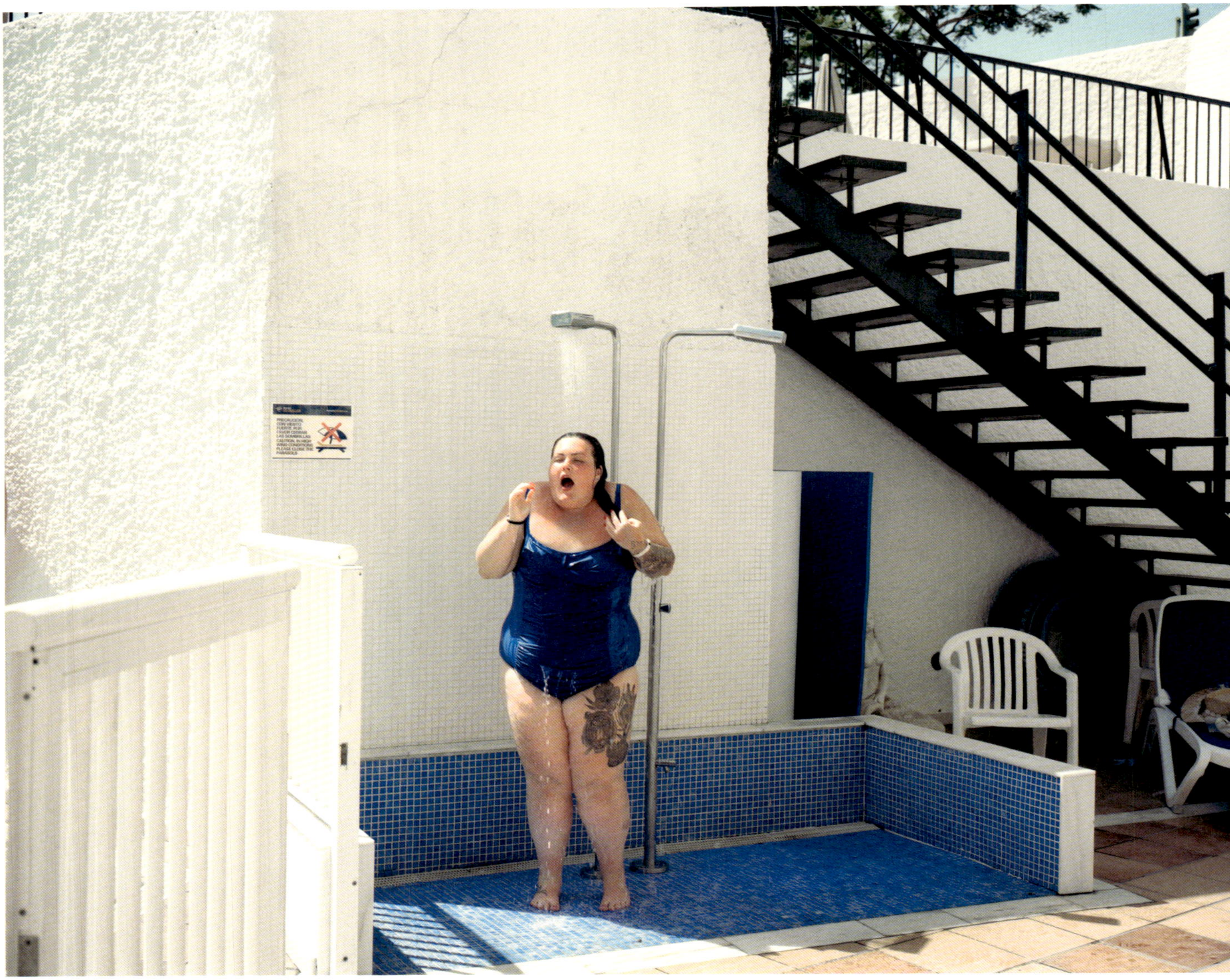

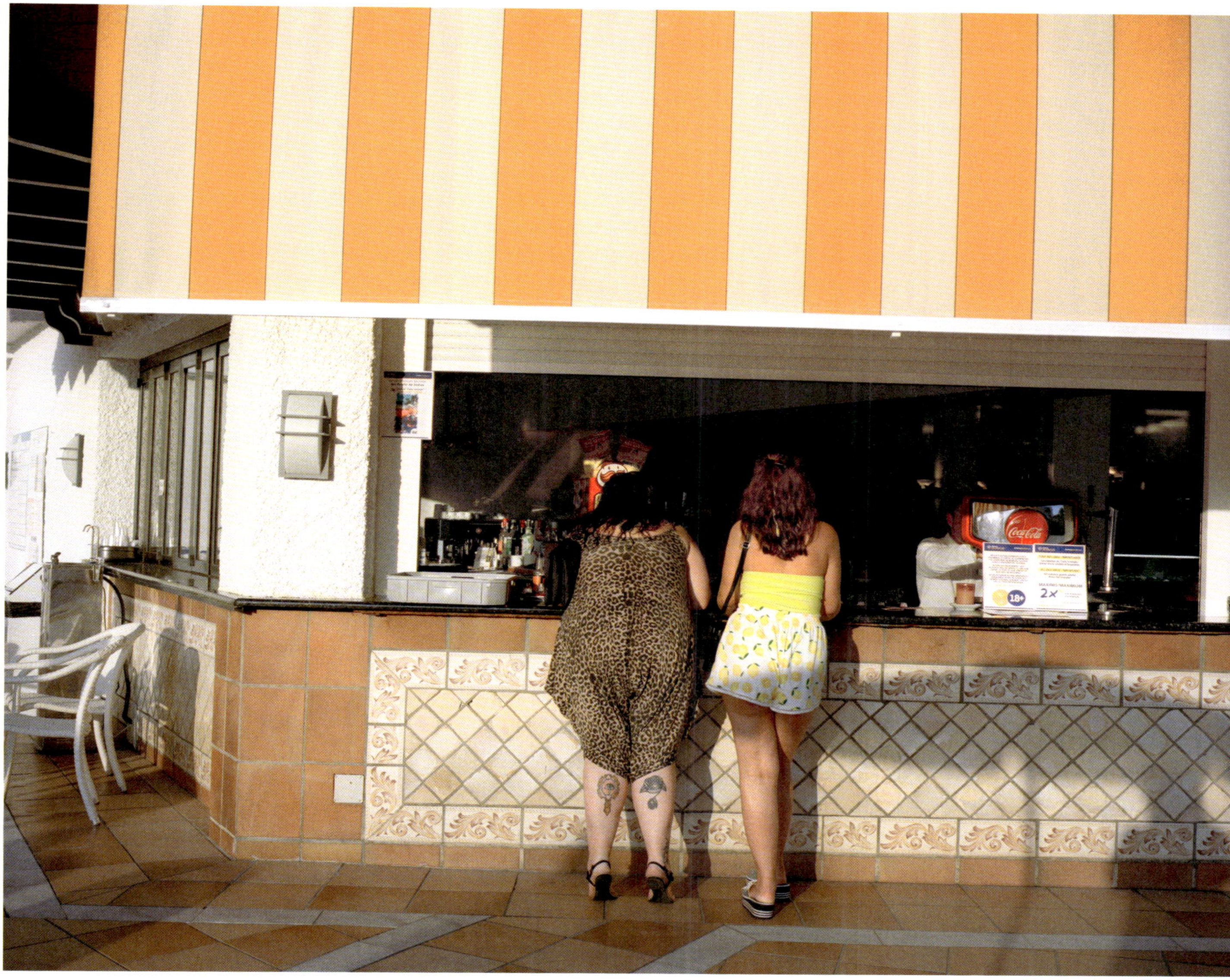
Coca-Cola
18+
2x

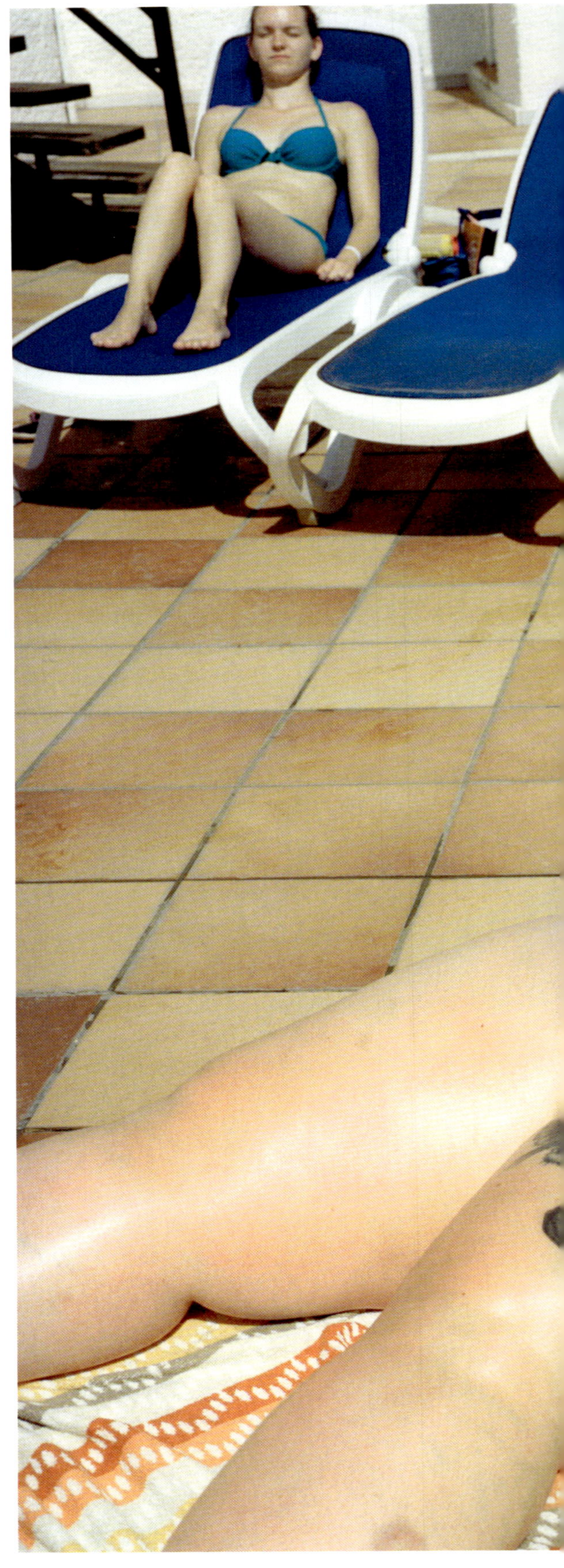

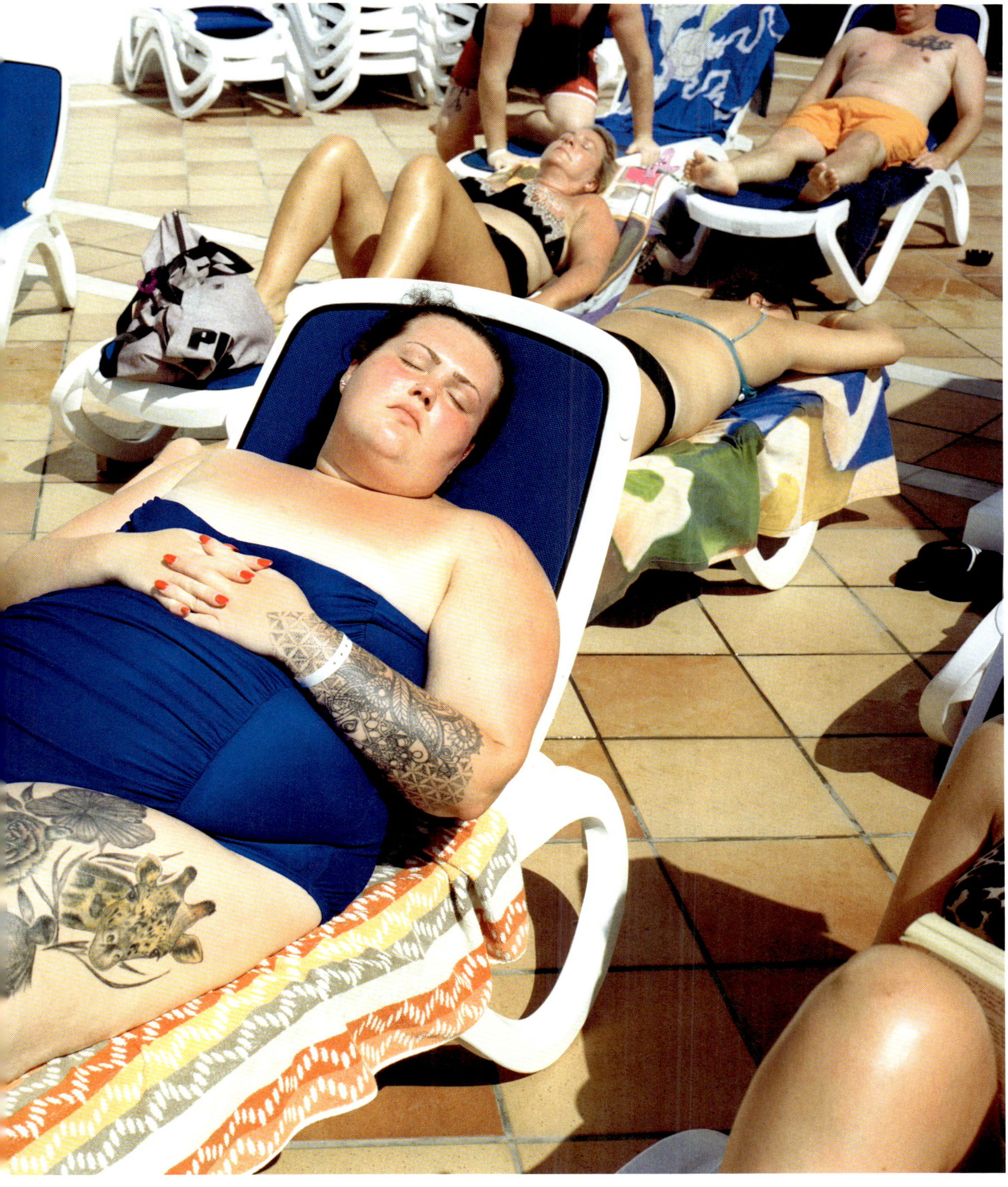

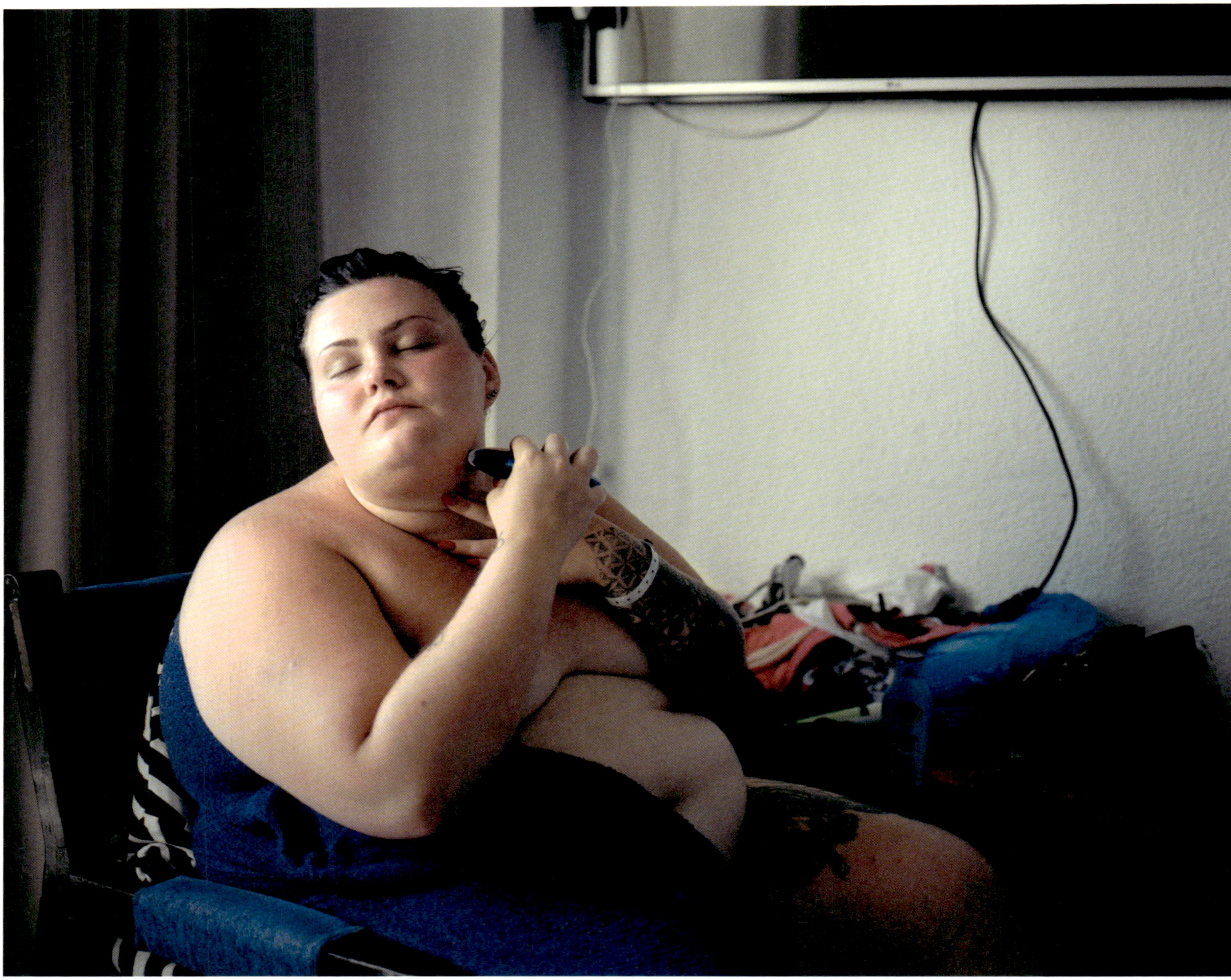

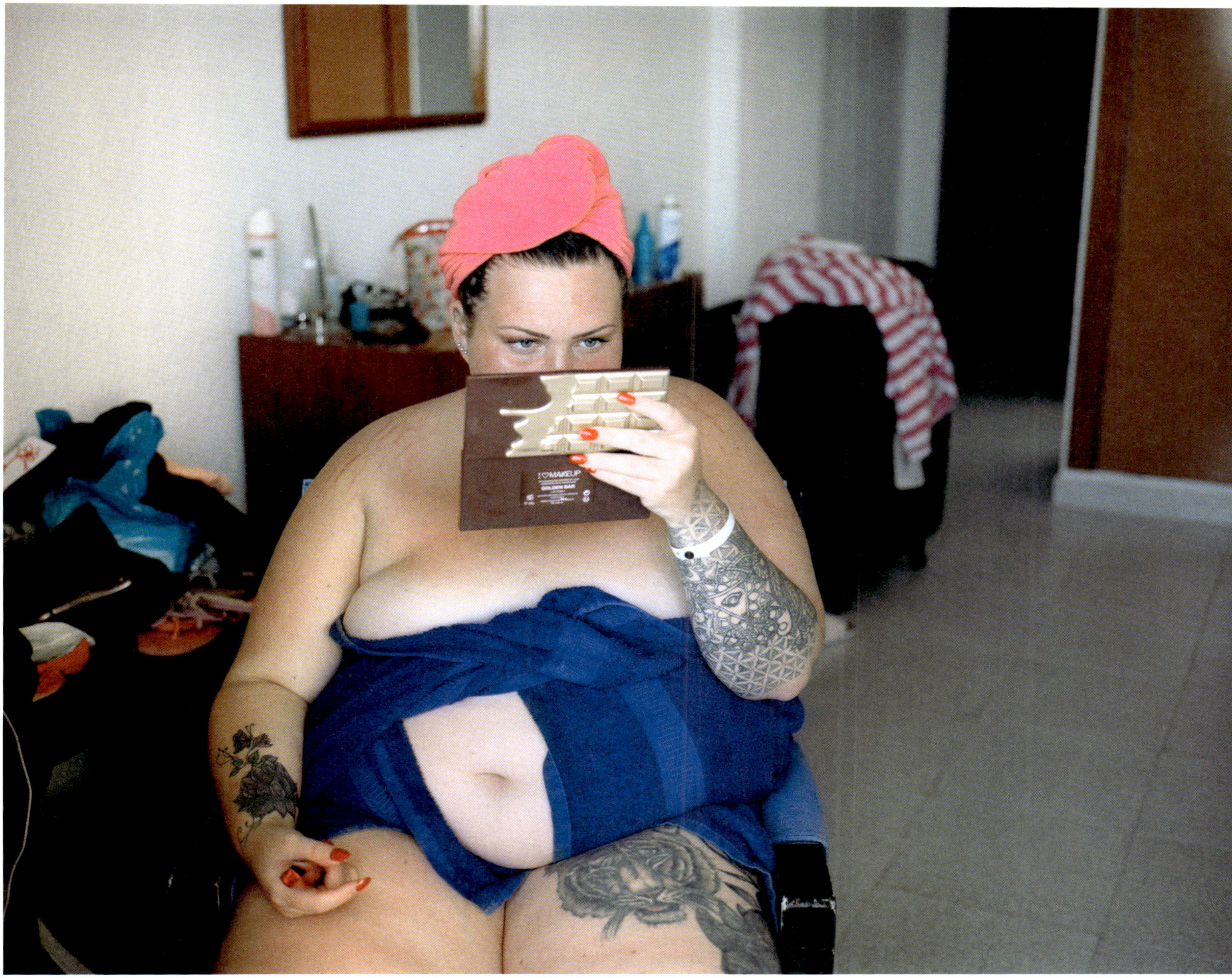
I ♡ MAKEUP
GOLDEN BAR

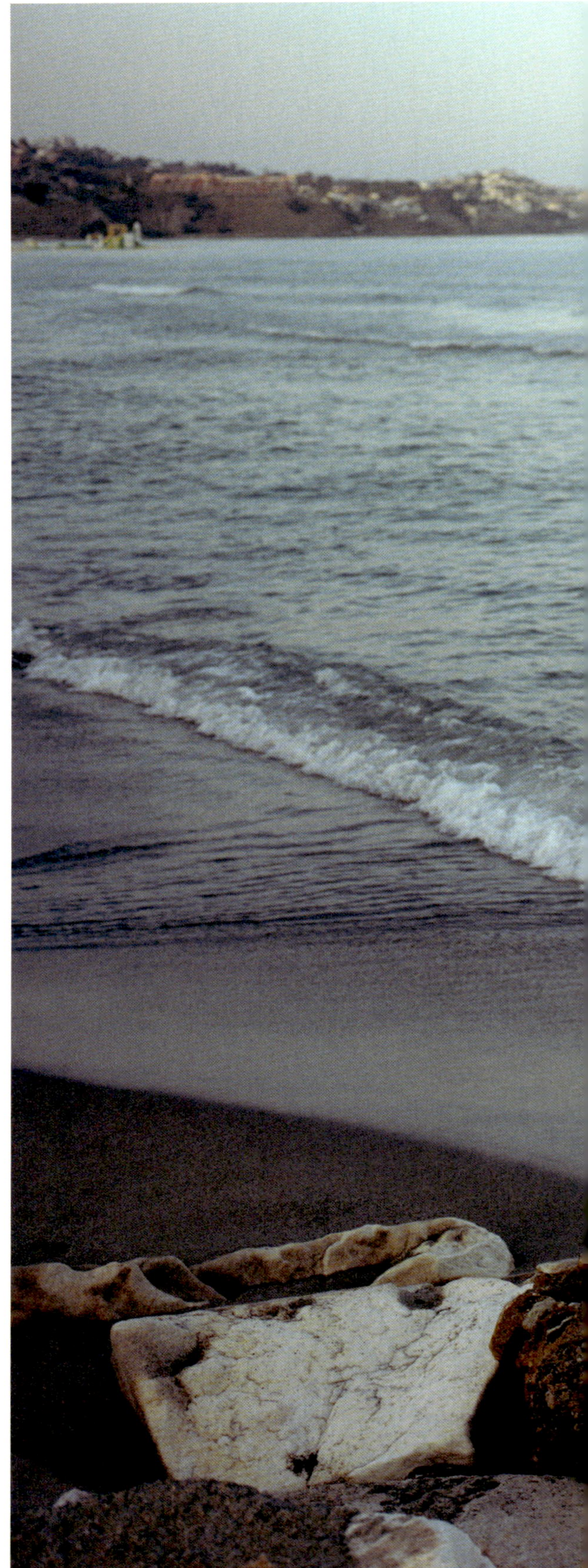

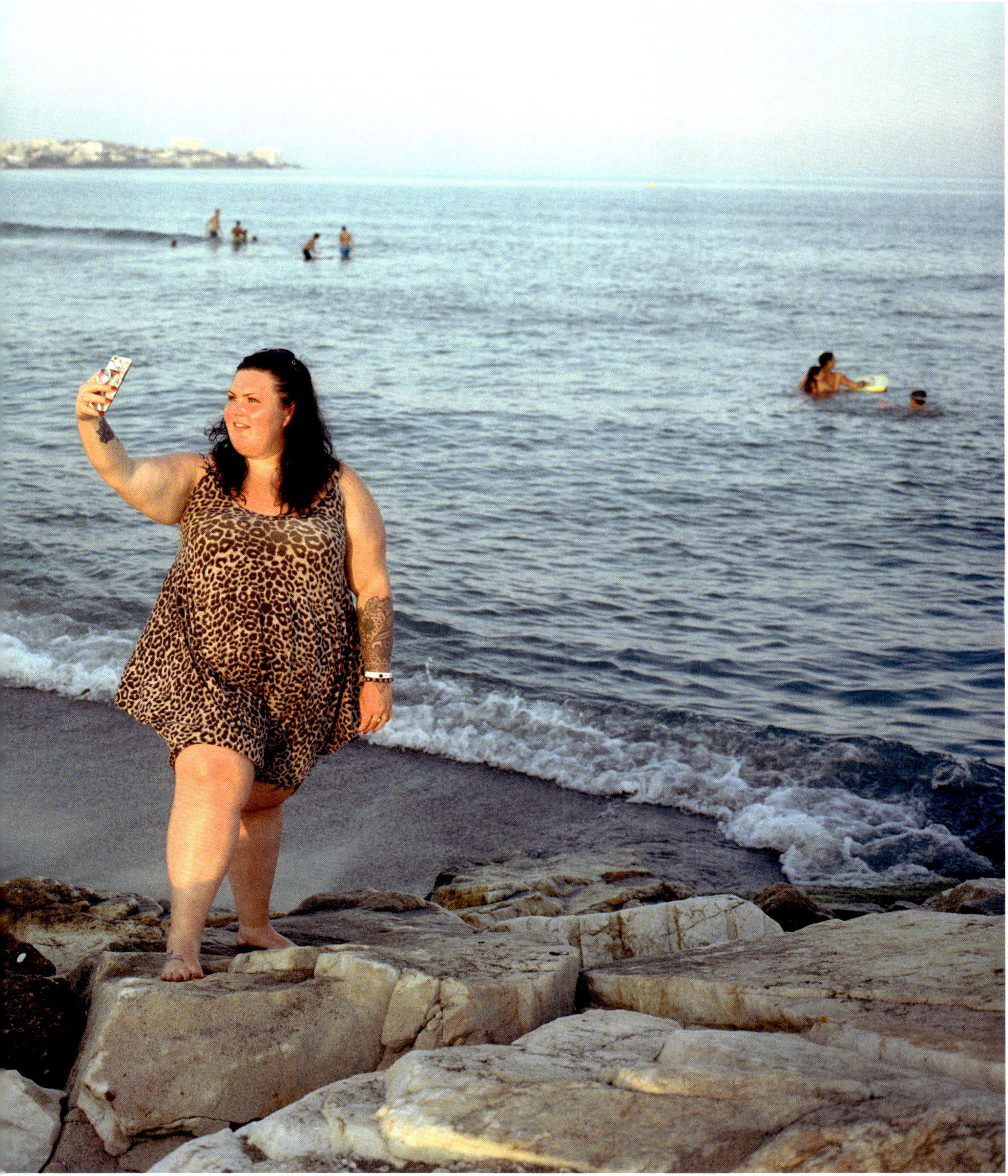

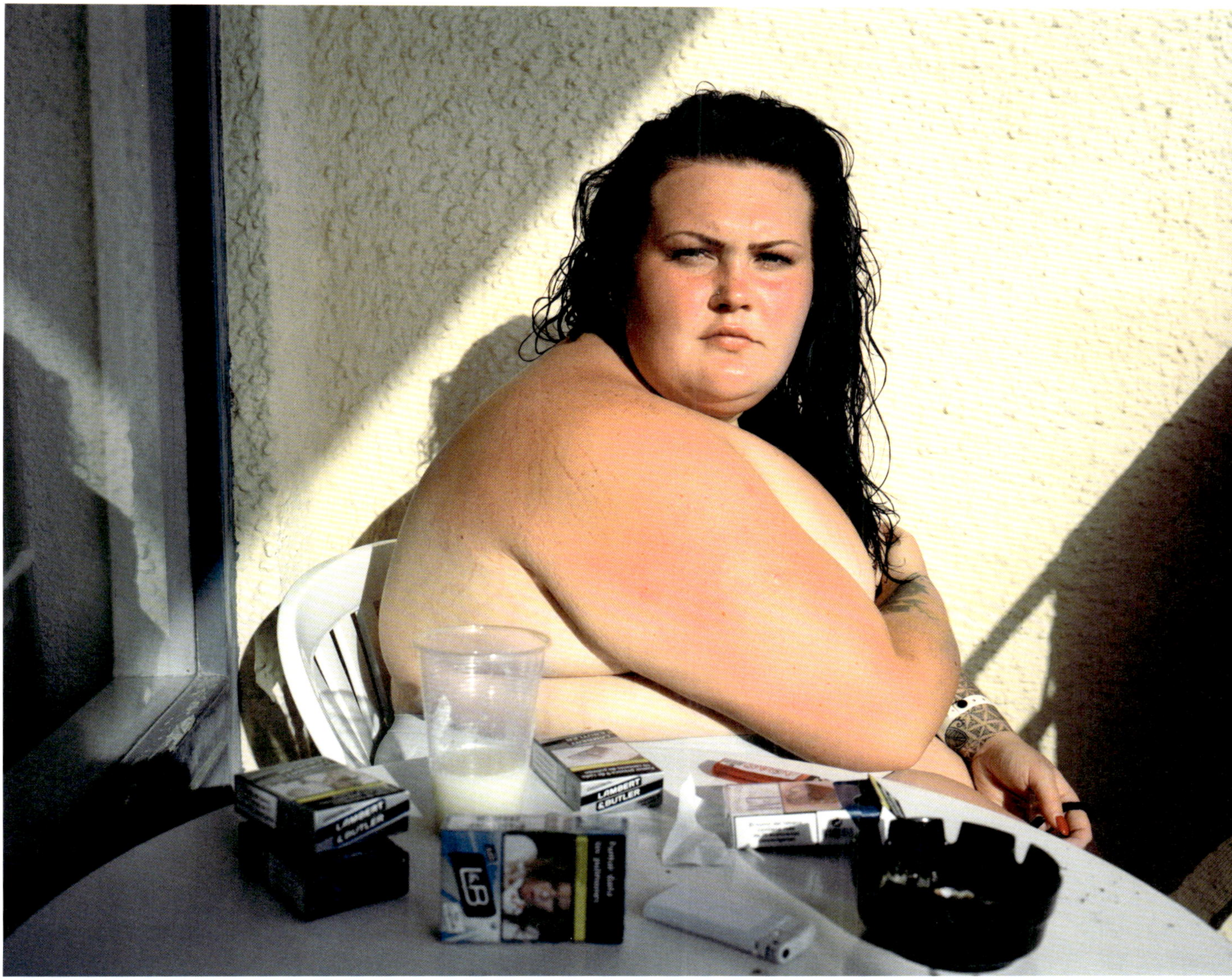
LAMBERT
&BUTLER

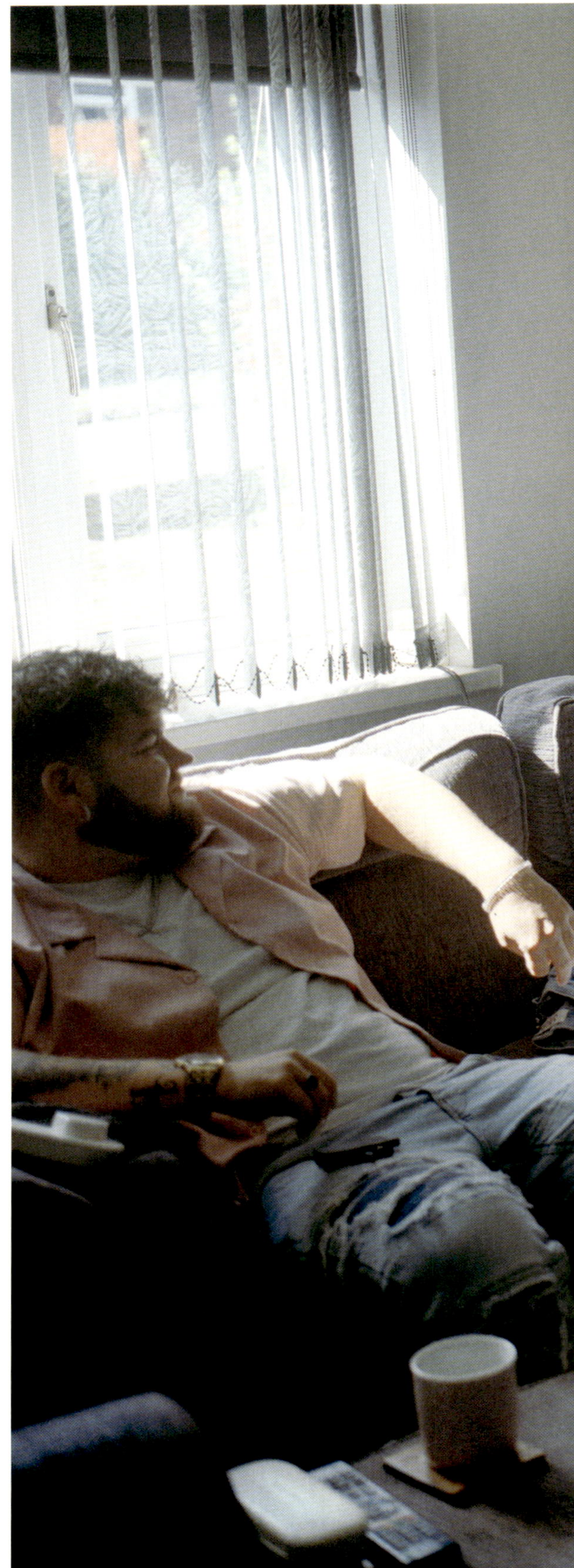

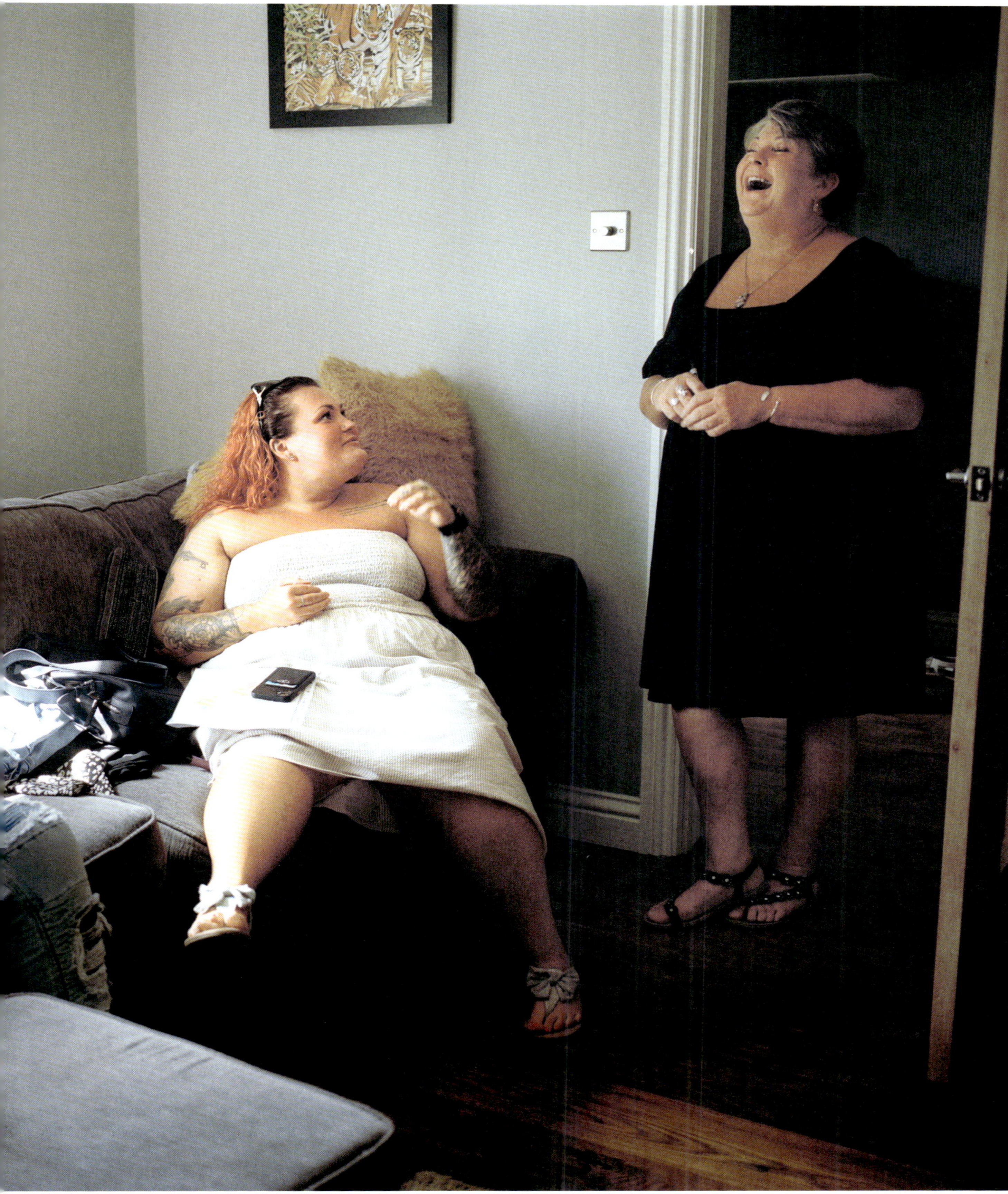

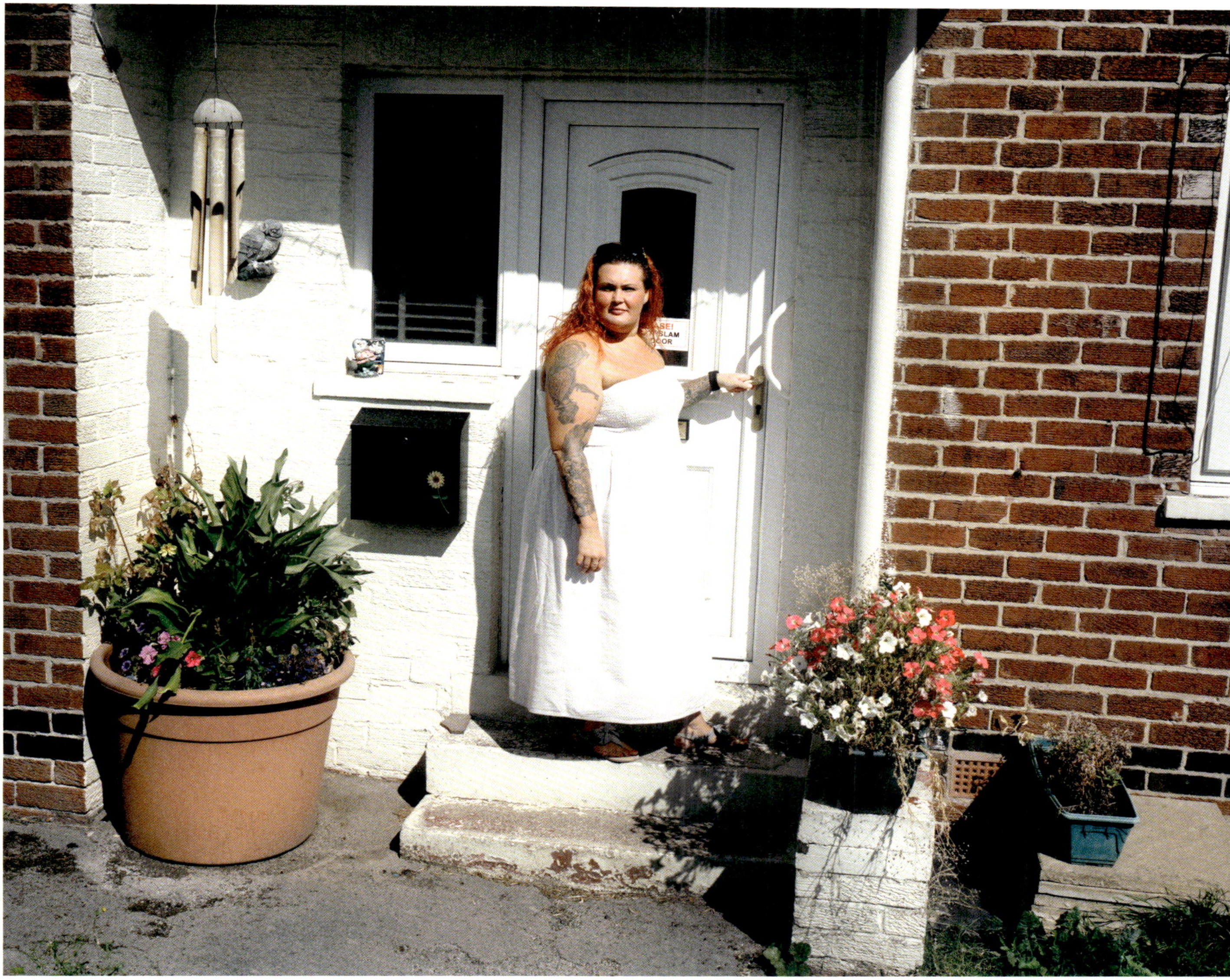

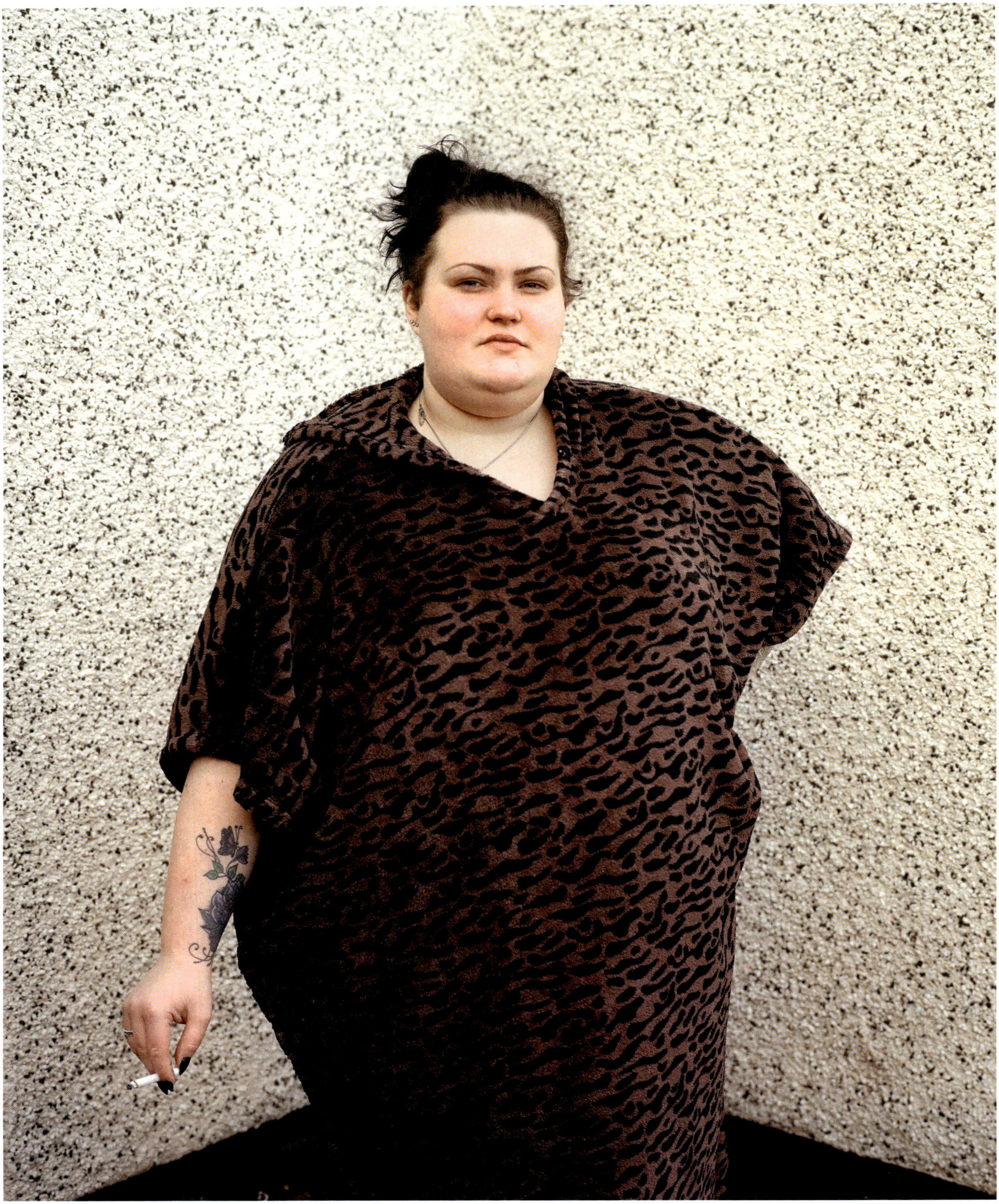

One in four people in England are obese.[1/2] Three decades ago, it was only about one in seven. Figures from Scotland, Northern Ireland and Wales follow a similar pattern. The UK is the fourth fattest country in Europe.[3]

Expanding waistlines can shorten lives. Today, in this country, obesity is a bigger killer than tobacco: it is an important factor in heart disease; type 2 diabetes; and being hit hard by Covid-19. The medical care costs of obesity to the NHS in 2014-2015 were estimated to be as high as £6.1bn. This is forecast to rise to £9.7bn per year by 2050.[4]

So, what has changed? Researchers point to long commutes, sedentary jobs, yo-yo dieting, sugary treats that beckon children in the shopping aisles, our electronic devices.

But obesity, often thought of as a failure of will and self restraint—'just eat less and move more'—has deep and complex roots. 'Much as not everybody can become an Olympic athlete, even with all the training in the world, not everybody has the capacity to become obese,' said Andrew Beamish, a consultant bariatric surgeon based in Swansea Bay University Health Board, south Wales and childhood obesity researcher. 'There has to be a certain biological set-up and that is largely genetic and partly acquired.'

Research shows the 'obesogenic environment'—the influences that promote obesity in individuals—starts in the womb. Pregnancy used to be seen as a time when weight gain was not only expected, but encouraged: 'Eat for two.' In fact studies show that women who gain 'excessive' weight during pregnancy are more likely to have heavy three-year-olds. Moreover, the risk of having overweight offspring increases with maternal BMI.

So what's wrong with putting on extra pounds as a baby? Aren't babies supposed to be chubby? According to Julie Lanigan, a dietician specialising in childhood nutrition at the UCL, Institute of Child Health and Great Ormond Street Hospital for Children, infants who grow rapidly are at higher risk of obesity through childhood. The heavy become heavier still. 'Once children get their dietary habits and lifestyle entrenched and start to gain weight, it's really difficult to reverse.'

It's clear that weight is not just a dietary issue. It's well-known that obesity is associated with socio-economic factors, such as under-employment or poverty. Circumstances often make it difficult for children and families to eat well. Poorer UK households would have to spend nearly half of their income to buy food for a healthy diet.[5] Fattening junk food, on the other hand, is affordable, heavily advertised, easily available and enticingly moreish. Fat, sugar and salt turn out to be the crucial elements in that particular factor. Research on rats proves that animals' brains react to sweet, fatty goods in the same way that addicts respond to cocaine.

Some experts are increasingly focusing on the hidden players to understand obesity. The biological drivers. For example, gut bacteria. The microbes in our intestines help us break down plant starches and fibres and yet their role appears to extend beyond digestion. New evidence indicates that gut bacteria alter the way we store fat, how we balance glucose in the blood, and how we respond to hormones that make us feel hungry or full. The wrong mix of microbes, it seems, can help set the stage for obesity from the moment of birth.

Hormones are also known to affect eating patterns. Leptin, which is produced by your body's fat cells, signals the brain to stop eating, helping to maintain your regular weight. First discovered in 1994, it is still early days of research. People with obesity produce a lot of leptin. However, they also tend to have a condition called leptin resistance: the brain doesn't see or recognise the leptin signal and thinks, wrongly, that it is starving.

People also rely on external cues, like portion size, to tell them when to stop eating. 'What we eat in any particular meal is, to a substantial degree, determined by what's in front of us,' explained Paul Rozin, a psychologist based at the University of Pennsylvania, in the United States, who published a paper in 2006 on 'unit bias'; a psychological phenomenon where no matter how large or small a particular item is—for example a sandwich or ice cream—we tend to view it as one portion. What's more, many portion sizes have increased from those recommended in the 1990s. A portion of garlic bread is now 30% larger; biscuits are on average 17% bigger. And for someone who is in the habit of eating a curry ready meal, it is twice as big as it was twenty years ago.[6] 'Bigger plates, bigger packs, bigger portions, bigger us. It's a nudge theory, encouraging us to consume more sugar, fat and calories than we ought to and making it much easier to do so,' said a spokesperson from the charity, Children's Food Campaign.

Then, there is dieting. We all know how hard it is to lose weight. Diets fail overwhelmingly often because they are very difficult to follow for any length of time. In a cruel twist, research suggests maintaining a healthy weight is even more difficult for people with obesity. 'There is this concept of the "body thermostat,"' said Andrew Beamish; an internal 'setpoint' that regulates our weight. 'Your setpoint for weight can increase very easily when you put on weight.' The body recognises the increased fat level and elevated weight as ideal and makes it the new setpoint. The result: even modest dieting and weight loss makes the body think it is going through starvation. 'But reducing it, turning the thermostat back down, so the body chases a lower weight, is almost impossible.'

The relationship between obesity and mental health is complex. Obesity is often driven by underlying mental health issues, and the shame and stigma of being overweight only compounds the problem, which, over time, leads to emotional and binge eating. 'We know that children use food as a coping mechanism,' said Kath Sharman, the founder of Shine Health Academy, a community-based weight management programme for ten to seventeen-year-olds, in Sheffield. 'They don't just eat when they're hungry, they eat when they're sad, miserable, if there's been an incident at school. The bullying is awful. One child had pins stuck in them to see whether they would pop because they were so round.'

High BMI and mental ill-health go increasingly hand-in-hand as children age, to create a combined health risk. Obesity at the age of seven is a risk factor for emotional distress at age eleven, and in turn, mental health problems predict a high BMI at age fourteen.[7]

William Dietz, director of the Stop Obesity Alliance at George Washington University, United States, and expert in pediatric obesity, stressed the importance of understanding obesity as a set of health issues. 'We talk about "people with obesity," not "obese people;" a phrasing that is more about identity.' From a medical point of view, he continued, 'obesity, like asthma, is something that happens to a person—a disease with many etiologies, not all of them well understood…Embedded in the stigmatisation of obesity is the idea that this is something that people have done to themselves; that is not the way to understand it.'

Sally Williams

1. The medical definition of obesity is based on BMI, the calculation of which is determined by weight and height. Obesity is classed as over 30; a healthy range is 18.5 to 24.9.
2. NHS Digital, digital.nhs.uk/data-and-information/publications/statistical/health-survey-for-england/2021/health-survey-for-england-2021-data-tables" Health Survey for England
3. https://apps.who.int/iris/bitstream/handle/10665/353747/9789289057738-eng.pdf
4. kingsfund.org.uk/sites/default/files/2021-07/Tackling%20obesity.pdf
5. foodfoundation.org.uk/press-release/major-report-highlights-impact-britains-disastrous-food-policy
6. bhf.org.uk/what-we-do/news-from-the-bhf/news-archive/2013/october/portion-distortion
7. cls.ucl.ac.uk/obesity-and-emotional-problems-tend-to-develop-together-as-children-age-new-research-shows/

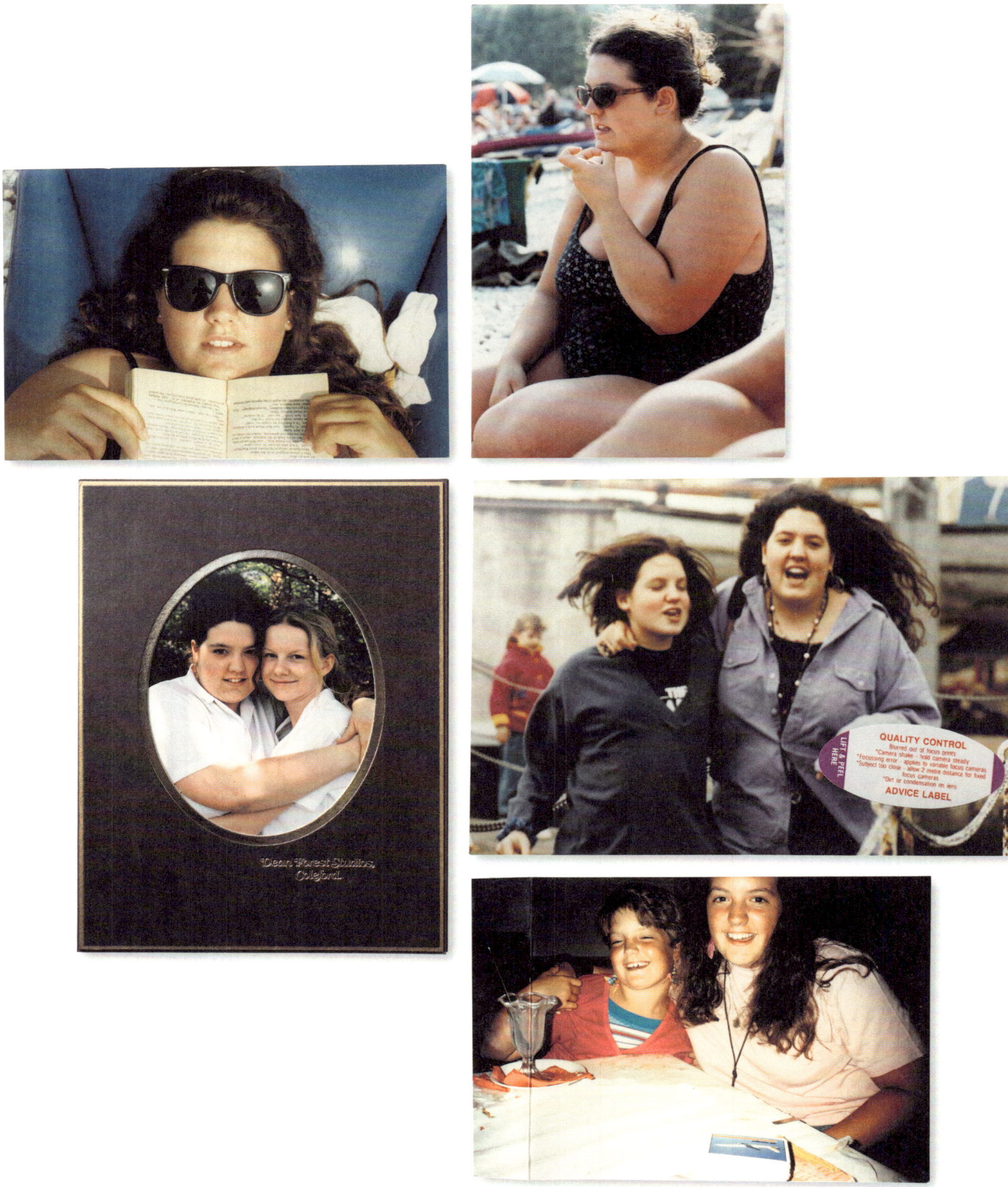

Photographs from the Trayler-Smith
family album, c. 1990s

‘I hope you lose weight, love Mark.’ That’s what the boy I had fancied for a year of junior school wrote in my leaving book. Seeing that summation of me in black and white, my spirit died.

At age eleven, I felt judged, criticised, and not approved of. He and others saw only my imperfect body, not the fact that I was funny and clever and warm. I came to believe that if I wasn’t fat, somehow everything else in my life would be problem-free. As I stepped into adolescence, all of this became my identity.

Fast forward to the age of thirty-three. I was working as a photographer at a press conference for a launch of health services to teenagers and there she was—Shannon, with a voice I had never found, reading a poem addressed to the professionals, pleading to be understood and not judged. I saw the mutuality between us and the difference.

She was the brave teenager I had never been able to be.

I saw a fourteen-year-old who was awkward, uncomfortable in her own (large) body; and within that there was also Shannon, who was a force of nature, already speaking out. This was the person who’s life I would travel with for the next twelve years. I would be there to see her first boyfriend, meet her fellow sprouting teenagers and listen to the classic family bickering. I observed the nerves of prom night and starting her first job. I was with her through the wayward times and when she began to find her way; discovering and creating meaning and purpose in her life.

We began slowly, working together with mutual understanding and care. Walking alongside Shannon, I could offer her a visual reflection as well as validation and approval. She could offer me insight. It felt like a perfect collaboration. The chemistry we shared was eventually able to flow and enlighten us both.

We shared so much over the years. Talking and listening to her revealed my own history. I began to see it reflected back to me in a new light—not just the boy who wrote those things at school but the way my Dad had always been desperate to see me ‘thin.’ Getting to know Shannon began to shed a light on thoughts, feelings and instincts I had been living with all my life. She revealed my history. And this gave me the courage to bring my teenage diaries out of the dark and to read them again. To share them and let them be seen here. To release myself from the shame within.

I am grateful for the trust Shannon placed in me and for the effect the work has had on both our lives.

The relationship between us has been reparative for me, because I have been able to see the person beyond the fat—Shannon was me. I have learned to view and experience myself beyond what people see, beyond their potential reductive perception of me, or indeed how I perceive or feel about myself. I find that liberating.

Through the making of this work, I have seen how shame has held me back from manifesting my true potential and purpose. The weight of shame kept me from getting to know myself, for a while. I’m now forty-five. And I’m more than okay. As is Shannon. It’s been a privilege to get to know us both.

Abbie Trayler-Smith

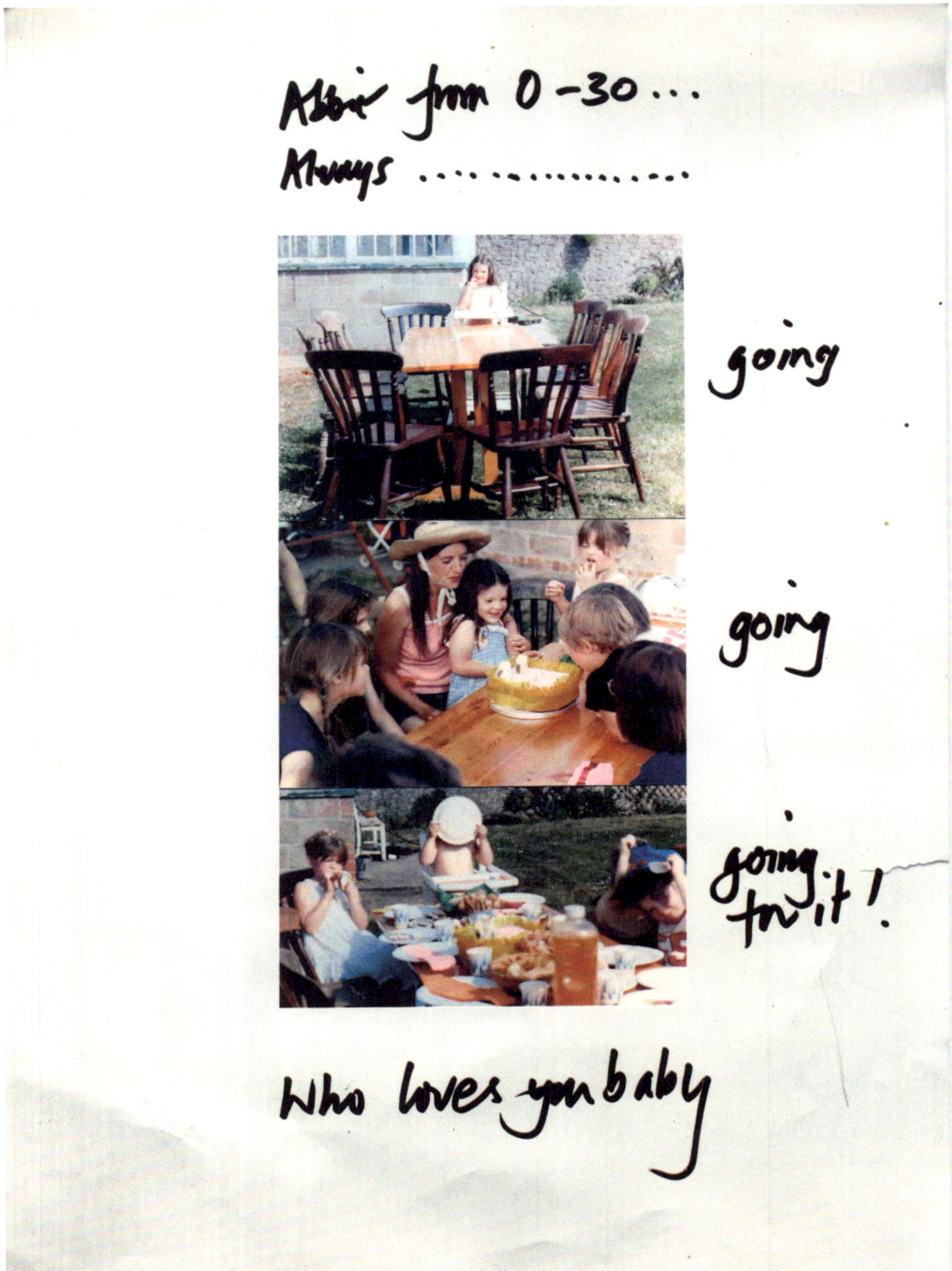

A thirtieth birthday card to Abbie from her parents showing three photographs of her from a past birthday party, being the first and the last at the table.

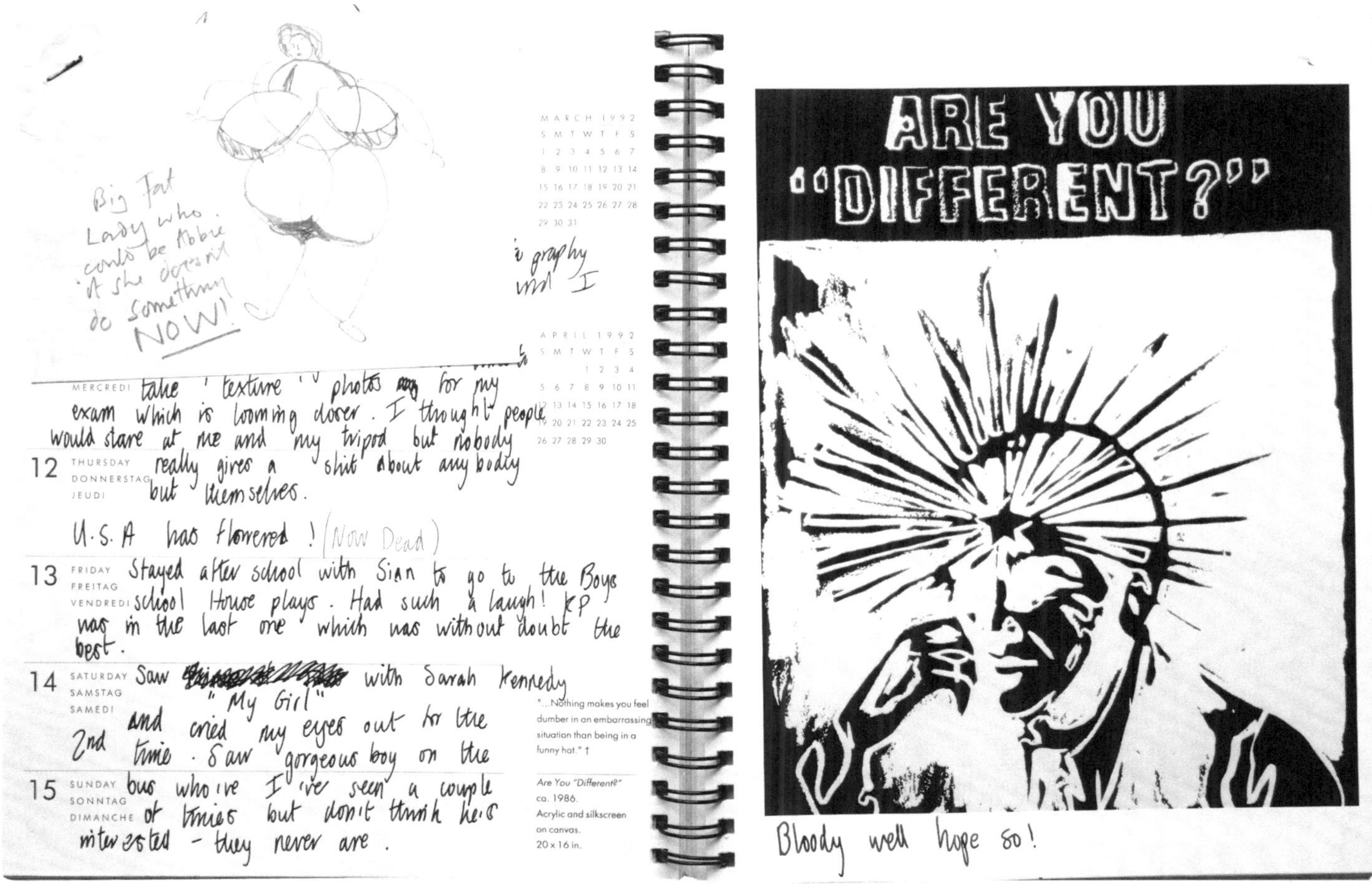

A drawing Abbie found from her father, stapled into her diary. It was a jokey warning about what would happen to her if she didn't lose weight 'NOW.' Age 14, 1991

1. Shannon, age 16, has the words 'Kiss it!' tattooed on her bottom as a message to the people who bullied her. Sheffield, 2013
3. Shannon, age 16, stands in her bedroom to record her 'before' picture on the eve of going into hospital for a gastric balloon as part of a medical trial at Sheffield Children's Hospital. Sheffield, 2013
7. Shannon, age 13, outside her home. This was the first photograph I made of her. Sheffield, 2013
9. Shannon, age 14, hanging out at a park in Rother Valley. Sheffield, 2011
11. Shannon, age 14, with her first boyfriend, James, in the woods near her home. Sheffield, 2011
12. Shannon, age 14, Sheffield, 2011
15. Shannon, age 15, hanging out with friends outside the local shops near her home. Sheffield, 2012
19. Shannon, age 15, with James, on a day trip to Rother Valley. Sheffield, 2011
21. Shannon, age 14, en route to school in year nine. Sheffield, 2010
22. A message received by Shannon on her blackberry at home. Sheffield, 2012
23. Shannon, age 15, watching her food intake at home. Sheffield, 2012
25. Shannon, age 21, with her Nannan and Grandad at their home. Sheffield, 2018
27. Shannon, age 21, at home. Sheffield, 2017
28. Shannon, 21, taking selfies at home. Sheffield, 2017
31. Shannon, age 17, with mum Lorraine at their home. Sheffield, 2014
32. Clothes hung up ready to try on. Sheffield, 2015
33. Shannon, age 15, tries on prom dresses at a specialist bridal shop. Barnsley, 2012
37. Shannon, age 15, en route to buy a prom dress. Barnsley, 2012
38. Shannon, age 15, getting her hair done for prom. Sheffield, 2012
41. Lorraine takes a picture of Shannon's hair as she leaves the salon, and heads home to get ready for prom. Sheffield, 2012
42. Shannon, age 15, applying makeup for prom night. Sheffield, 2012
43. Shannon, age 15, arriving at prom. Sheffield, 2012
44. Shannon, age 15, and her friends get out of the limo to walk into prom night. Sheffield, 2012
47. Shannon, age 15, laughing with friends at prom. Sheffield, 2012
48. Shannon, age 22, in her first flat. Sheffield, 2018
51. Shannon, age 16, recovers in hospital after an operation to have a gastric balloon inserted into her stomach, at Sheffield Children's Hospital. Sheffield, 2013
53. Shannon, age 21, hanging out the laundry. Sheffield, 2018
54. Shannon, age 26, hanging out with her best friend, Emily, at Emily's home. Sheffield, 2022
55. Shannon, age 24, with her first boyfriend, James, who she reunited with. Sheffield, 2020
56. Shannon, age 21, at her family home. Sheffield, 2018
59. Shannon, age 21 and Lorraine. Sheffield, 2018
61. Shannon, age 22. Sheffield, 2019
62. Shannon, age 22, getting ready for a night out to see Chocolate Men theatre production. Sheffield, 2018
65. Shannon, age 21, at home. Sheffield, 2018
66. Shannon, age 21, at home. Sheffield, 2018
67. Shannon, age 21, with James, at his flat. Sheffield, 2018
69. Shannon, age 21, with James, outside his home. Sheffield, 2018
70. Shannon, age 16, near her home. Sheffield, 2013
73. Shannon, age 19, getting ready for her birthday party. Sheffield, 2015
74. Shannon, age 19, at the tattoo shop. Sheffield, 2015
76. Shannon, age 19, at her birthday party. Sheffield, 2015
77. Shannon, age 19, at her birthday party. Sheffield, 2015
78. Shannon, age 21, on a night out. Sheffield, 2018

81-97. Shannon, age 22, on holiday. Costa del Sol, Spain, 2018

98. Shannon, age 26, with Lorraine and brother Kieran, at their family home. Sheffield, 2022
101. Shannon, age 26, leaves her mum's house. Sheffield, 2022
102. Shannon, age 22, in her first flat. Sheffield, 2018

Acknowledgements

The Waltons: Shannon, mum Lorraine and brother Kieran, for letting me into your family, for your honesty and openness, for the laughs, the tears and everything in-between.

Kath Sharman, child and adolescent therapist and founder of Shine, for your tireless and inspiring work in obesity management for children. I can't thank you enough for your invaluable help, support and warmth over the years.

Claudine Boeglin of Dandy Vagabonds for the vision to create: www.thebigoproject.com along with Jérôme Guckenheim, Gianluca Alla and Marina Vitaglione: for this beautiful website made with love in lockdown.

Justin Sutcliffe, for being the 'Jedi.' And for your patience and encouragement in making me a kick ass kickstarter film.

Sally Williams, Cole Moreton, for your sense and sensibility.

Caroline Cortizo: it's a priviledge.

Stuart and Gemma and all the team at GOST: My heartfelt thanks.

The Emma's: Sian Davey, Clémentine Schneidermann, Lua Ribeira, Alys Tomlinson and Alice Zoo, I love our challenging and stimulating dialogue. Martin Parr and all at the Martin Parr Foundation for hosting us and the ongoing support.

Harry Borden for encouraging me to get this idea off the ground.

Anna Stevens, Valeria Cardi, Josh Lustig, Paula James, Michael Regnier and Adrian Evans of Panos Pictures, Chelsea Wild, Emma Hinchliffe, Zoe Burge, Katharine Price, Maggie Gudmundsson, Francesca Sears, Fiona Rogers, Zelda Cheatle, Artur Tixiliski, Chris Ashman, Adam Loveridge, Alessia Glaviano, James O Jenkins, Kajal Patel, Sunil Shah, Sarah Le Brocq, John Wyatt-Clarke, James Gerrard-Jones, Sarah Shenker, Dom Tyler, Ben Smith, Christiane Monarchi, Helena Velez Olabarria, Ines Casals and Silvia Omedes, Yumi Goto, Christopher Morris, Oli Williams, Sophie Batterbury, Cheryl Newman, Sharon O'Neill, Amy Christian, Eleanor Farmer, Tove Spissøy Gerhardsen, Jakob Jakobsen, Daniella Zalcman and all at Women Photograph, Ben Gilbert and The Wellcome Collection, Paul Sampson and Oriel Colwyn, Will Troughton and The National Library of Wales, IdeasTap Magnum, The The Taylor Wessing Photographic Portrait Prize, The National Portrait Gallery (UK) and World Press Photo.

My son, Florian Borden, for everything.

And lastly, my mum and dad and sister Chloe, for loving me always.

Kiss it!
First published in 2023
by GOST Books, London

info@gostbooks.com
gostbooks.com

Edited and designed by GOST:
Rossella Castello, Katie Clifford, Gemma Gerhard,
Justine Hucker, Allon Kaye, Eleanor Macnair,
Claudia Paladini, Ana Rocha

Image reproduction by Shifting Pixels:
Caroline Cortizo, Samantha Humble-Smith

Printed in Italy by EBS

British Library cataloguing-in-publication
data. A catalogue record of this book is available
from the British Library.

ISBN 978-1-910401-95-8